HANDGUNNER'S GUIDE

Handgunner's Guide

Including the Art of the Quick-Draw and Combat Shooting

BY CHIC GAYLORD

COACHWHIP PUBLICATIONS
GREENVILLE, OHIO

To
LYN WHERRY GAYLORD

A tender comrade, loyal friend and understanding wife. Without her devoted help this book could not have been written.

Handgunner's Guide, by Chic Gaylord
© 2024 Coachwhip Publications edition

First published 1960
Charles 'Chic' Gaylord, 1914-1992
CoachwhipBooks.com

ISBN 1-61646-585-9
ISBN-13 978-1-61646-585-8

CONTENTS

Introduction	7
Acknowledgments	11
Preface — Our Handgun Heritage	15
CHAPTER 1 Adapting Your Gun	17
CHAPTER 2 Weapons for Concealment	29
CHAPTER 3 Personal Defense Weapons	35
CHAPTER 4 Service Weapons	39
CHAPTER 5 Guns for Combat Practice	45
CHAPTER 6 The Fun Guns	49
CHAPTER 7 Centerfire Hunting Weapons	56
CHAPTER 8 Ammunition	63

CHAPTER 9 Undercover Holsters	73
CHAPTER 10 Concealment Holsters	77
CHAPTER 11 Service Holsters	85
CHAPTER 12 Field Holsters	89
CHAPTER 13 Western Holsters	91
CHAPTER 14 Commercial Targets	95
CHAPTER 15 Safe Gun Handling	99
CHAPTER 16 Close Combat Shooting	102
CHAPTER 17 Alley Cleaning	107
CHAPTER 18 Mid-Range Combat	109
CHAPTER 19 Long-Range Shooting	115
CHAPTER 20 Quick Draw	117
CHAPTER 21 The Psychology of Gun Fighting	147
CHAPTER 22 Holster History	151
CHAPTER 23 The Shooting Gallery	161
Index	171

INTRODUCTION

THIS IS A BOOK by a man who knows his business. Chic Gaylord has the hand of a craftsman, the eye of an artist, and the mind of a research scientist.

Chic makes holsters as a business, and, as a hobby, he seeks to improve his products. An excellent combination for a successful business, but Chic's research-oriented mind has probed far beyond the holster, to the gun and gunfighting. Today, Chic Gaylord is "top gun" in the world of combat shooting.

Chic was raised in Delta County, Colorado, an area opened up for settlement by the six-gun, the old Peacemaker of frontier days. His parents and neighboring ranchers often spoke of guns and gunfights. In these friendly discussions Chic listened to every word and then discussed the finer points with an uncle who had witnessed quite a few gunfights and, it was rumored, had also participated in a few of them. At an early age Chic was not only indoctrinated in the use of handguns, but also given a fine appreciation of their ability to bring sudden death.

His family packed him off to study at the University of Nebraska, where he majored in art. Success in his studies led to an instructor's post at the Grand Central School of Art in New York City. His creative mind outdid his brush and he became an idea man for Peter Arno, the dean of American cartoonists. After thirteen years with Arno, Chic thought he could see greener fields in the public-relations business and left to join a firm of Broadway and Hollywood public-relations consultants.

Then, almost accidentally, Chic started to make holsters. His latent interest in firearms was coming to the surface and since it was now supported by his artistic sense of motion and line, Chic began to turn out holsters that were different from what might be termed "store-bought" holsters.

Soon good-will advertising by satisfied customers had "seeded" Gaylord holsters in Latin America, the West, the deep South, and almost every major American city. Chic is proud that he does not advertise, but his customers and his holsters do a lot of advertising for him.

The mind that for thirteen years gave Pete Arno ideas for many of his *New Yorker* cartoons, and which helped Chic in the highly competitive field of public relations, went beyond holster design and manufacture to the guns and the people who use them. He started a "job analysis" of the circumstances under which various types of police officers and other law-enforcement agents carry and use their weapons. In a year he had systematically compiled his collected data and designed holsters to meet the basic needs of almost every type of law-enforcement agent or officer. He wasn't satisfied until he stocked sixty different holsters.

From this level it was just a simple step to a more detailed analysis of the actual situations that lead to gunfights.

Chic's contacts with law-enforcement agents have been very extensive, and through them he brings to combat shooting the thinking of men who live with a gun twenty-four hours a day, seven days a week, month in and month out. If the Rockefeller or Ford Foundation had furnished some scientist with a grant of funds to pursue studies in the field of combat shooting, I don't think the procedure would have differed very much from Chic Gaylord's day-to-day learning and thinking. His shop on Manhattan's West Forty-seventh Street is daily turned into an experimental laboratory. Many of his customers are men who have been in gunfights with well-armed opponents seeking to kill them, and they talk to Chic. Possibly he sells this man a holster, or plans a new one to fit that one's particular need, but, more important, he classifies and catalogues the information he secures from these individuals — the living "experts" in this field because of their survival.

Chic's questioning sometimes sounds like a district attorney quizzing a defendant, at other times like that of a psychiatrist probing the mind of a patient. Chic doesn't confine his probing to the mechanical aspects of a gun fight; he attempts to find out the thinking of the man looking down an opponent's gun barrel. Was he prepared mentally to face a life-or-death situation?

As Chic's fame spread, his normal law-enforcement customers were joined by a few European and Latin American governmental agents who might be loosely grouped as "bodyguards" to various heads of governments. Many of these men had also survived armed conflict, and in conversation with them Chic added to his increasing knowledge of sudden death.

Of course, as a holster manufacturer Chic Gaylord had a vested interest in both psychological and physical factors which would assist an individual in getting a handgun into action without delay, but Chic's interest was that of a scientist attempting to prove a new concept.

Now in the pages of this book we have new concepts in gunfighting, and we have evidence and proof. Chic reveals why some of the great figures of the Old West were slow on the draw just that "once" necessary to end up on Boot Hill; and why a policeman hesitates, loses to an armed criminal, and ends up as the central figure in an awe-inspiring "inspector's" funeral.

Starting with the basic psychology of gunfighting, Chic has gone on to "souping up" guns and holsters. The Gaylord models improve the basic factory design of the weapon and the holster's design will be keyed to one of three major factors: (1) speed, (2) concealment, or (3) safety. Gun "butchery," as it is sometimes termed, does speed up gun handling, and the custom designs of holsters fit the demands of a man's job. An undercover narcotic agent's vital concern must be concealment; an off-duty policeman's worry is usually safety; and a "bodyguard's" concern is speed.

Chic was one of the early exponents of wax bullets, which now make quick-draw practice safe. He also assisted in the design of an electrical apparatus for timing the speed of a draw. And he went one step further and designed a combat silhouette target scaled down to permit close-range practice with these harmless projectiles. The result is that Chic combined safe quick-draw practice, accurately timed, with accuracy of gun handling.

During my last eight years with the New York Police Department I carried a gun "souped up" according to Chic's best advice, in a variety of holsters, each one keyed to my job at the time. I shot it a great deal on the pistol range but never had to shoot it in combat. I've had it "out" on more than one occasion, but something about my draw, or the gun itself, seemed to communicate very effectively. I thank Chic for his thousands of words of good advice and I believe, with him, that opponents don't "call" an adversary prepared to shoot to kill, if warranted.

Any individual interested in shooting as a hobby, any law-enforcement agent concerned with defensive firing, and those persons who look upon gunfighting as a fascinating aspect of early frontier history will find in this book the exact rudiments necessary for understanding this type of individual combat.

Gaylord's unconfusing language and his step-by-step presentation of material make this an enjoyable book to read and understand. This is truly a book by a man who knows his business — *thoroughly*.

> PAUL B. WESTON
> *Deputy Chief Inspector*
> New York City Police Department
> (Retired)

ACKNOWLEDGMENTS

I WISH TO TAKE this opportunity to express my sincere gratitude to the following men and organizations without whose information, assistance, and friendship throughout the years this book could never have been written:

Lieutenant Robert Pardua, of the New York Police Department's Ballistics Bureau; Deputy Chief Inspector Paul B. Weston, retired; Detective Harry Fritz, retired; Detective John Tonner, retired; Detective Vincent Heffernan; Detective Frank Malerba; Detective Joseph Suarez; Captain Thomas Rannahan; Lieutenant John J. Murphy; Lieutenant Arthur Schultheiss; Lieutenant Alex Kaplan; Detective Robert Ellison; Detective Joseph Garahan; Detective Reno Ganio; Lieutenant Earl Campozzi; Detective William Graff; Detective Vincent Wilson; Patrolman William Cash; Patrolman Donald Arrington; Patrolman William Spaeth; Patrolman Frank Lannert; and Patrolman Donald Pagani, all of the New York Police Department.

The late Inspector Frank Monaco, and the late Inspector John Novak of the United States Bureau of Immigration.

Field Supervisor Charles Siragussa; District Supervisor John Cusak; Special Agents Eugene J. Marshall, Larry Katz, George O'Connor, Rudy Mercado, and the late James A. "Pat" Patterson, all of the United States Treasury Department's Bureau of Narcotics.

Pennsylvania State Trooper Philip Melley, killed in the line of duty.

Sergeant Ralph Smith of the New York State Police.

Special Agents Dean Hatfield, Buck Sample, and Nick Kalmes of the Federal Bureau of Investigation.

Leslie Smith, special agent in charge of the Ballistics Bureau, Florida State sheriff's office.

Bill Donovan, vice-president, and Bill Henry, sales manager, of the High Standard Manufacturing Company, Hamden, Connecticut; Bill Ruger and Harry Siefried of Sturm Ruger & Co., Inc., Southport, Connecticut; "Goody" Goodwin and Bill Maloney of the Colt's Patent Fire Arms Manufacturing Company, Hartford, Connecticut; Douglas Hellstrom of Smith & Wesson, Springfield, Massachusetts; Joe and Ted Tonkin of the Continental Arms Corporation, New York City; Joe Gaydos; Al Giza; Don Parker; Herbert "Longo" Garrison; Carl Estey; and Joseph L. Gaylord.

Lucian Cary, *True* Magazine; Pete Kuhlhoff, *Argosy;* Ed Wallace, New York *World Telegram & Sun;* Larry Koller, *Guns & Hunting;* the late Meyer Berger, New York *Times;* Elmer Keith, *Guns;* David O. Moreton, *Law & Order;* Stan Smith; Sid Latham, Metro Group; Dorian St. George, Carling's Conservation Club; and Kermit Jaedecker, New York *Daily News*.

The rare photographs of frontier gun fighters are from the Mercaldo Archive, 119-04 Liberty Avenue, Richmond Hill 19, New York.

The photos of antique revolvers are from the Colt Collection, Hartford, Connecticut.

I wish to thank Werner Kuhn and Martin Dall for their photographic assistance, and express a special thank you to David B. Eisendrath, Jr., for his outstanding contribution of the photographs in Chapter 20, and his many other fine photos throughout the book.

CHIC GAYLORD

HANDGUNNER'S GUIDE

PREFACE
Our Handgun Heritage

THE HANDGUN has always played a vital role in the history of this nation. "The Shot Heard Round the World" was fired from one of a pair of Scottish flintlock pistols at the Battle of Lexington. The single-action Army Model Colt revolver brought law and order to our western frontier in the 1870's, and General George A. Patton brought law and order to Nazi Germany when wearing a pair of these historic handguns in the 1940's. The first practical revolvers were manufactured in Paterson, New Jersey. In the hands of the Texas Rangers much of the early history of the Lone Star State was written with the "Texas Paterson Colt" revolver. During the Civil War the revolver really came into its own. Its effectiveness in cavalry engagements virtually made the saber obsolete as a serious weapon of warfare. The possession of a cap-and-ball revolver — whether it was a Whitney, Man-

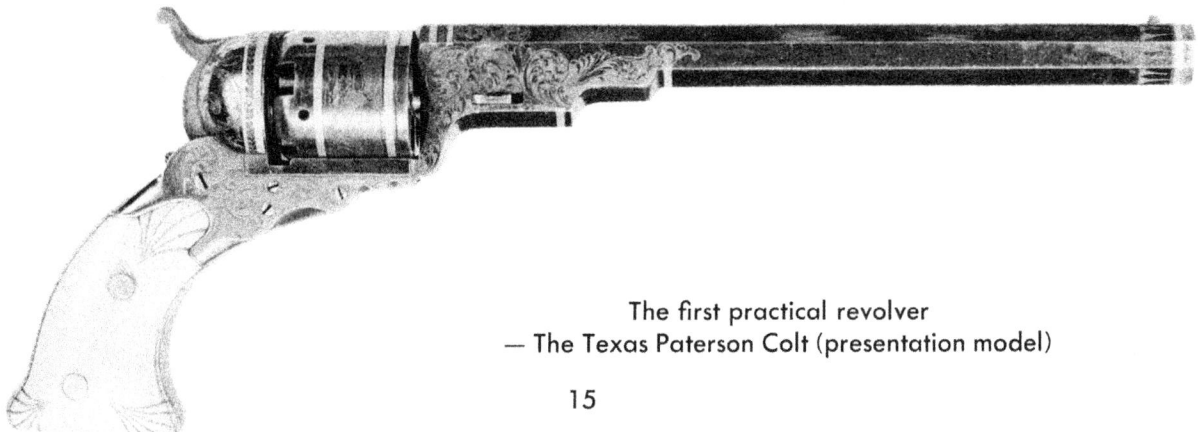

The first practical revolver
— The Texas Paterson Colt (presentation model)

hattan, Star, or preferably a Remington or Colt — was just about the best kind of life insurance an infantryman could have, no matter which side he was fighting on. On the bloody Kansas-Missouri border, the six-gun became a way of life. In the hands of the cavalry, vigilance committees, and "hanging Judge Parker's" army of deputy United States marshals, the revolver made the postwar West safe and fit for human habitation. The Wells Fargo Colt was the sole protection of youths who rode the Pony Express. Colt revolvers safeguarded the lives of the men girding the continent with the telegraph and the railroad.

Colt revolvers in the hands of Teddy Roosevelt's Rough Riders blazed a path of glory up San Juan Hill and brought to a close the century in which the invention of the Colt revolver had as great a social and economic effect on our nation as the invention of the airplane and the Model T Ford were to have in the century that followed.

With the exception of John Mose Browning, the genius of Ogden, Utah, the finest firearms designers and inventors in the world emerged from the countless arms companies that mushroomed along the Connecticut River Valley. Most of the world's arms were either designed by or copied from weapons conceived by these inspired gunsmiths. (Although most semi-automatic pistols are basically American in design we are inclined to regard them as foreign.)

The revolver, however, is as thoroughly and completely American as turkey for Thanksgiving. Today the handgun is the primary weapon of peace officers in their war against crime. The handgun in the glove compartment of your car, in the holster at your side, in the bedside table of your home can be the ultimate guarantee of your own safety and the safety of those dependent upon you. As long as we defend our constitutional right to this safeguard of our freedom we will remain free.

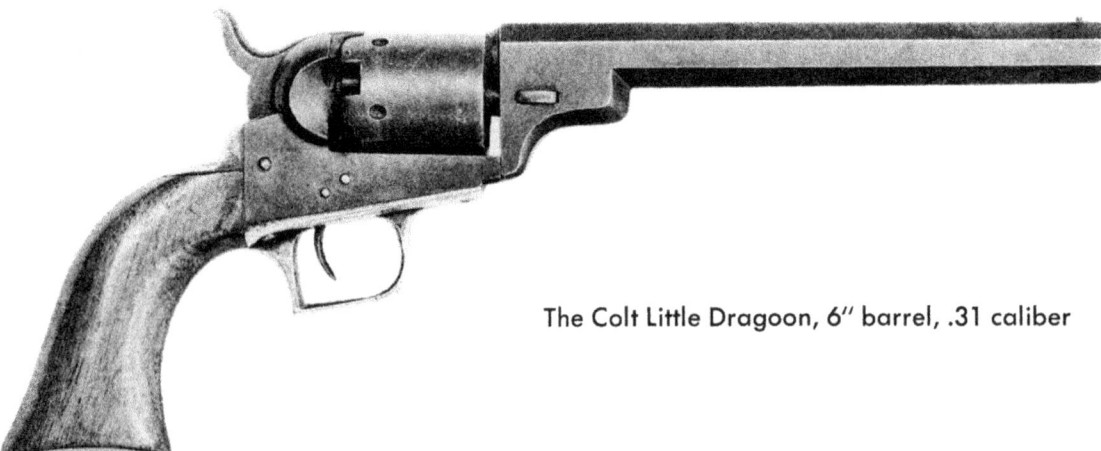

The Colt Little Dragoon, 6" barrel, .31 caliber

CHAPTER 1

Adapting Your Gun

Handguns are manufactured with grips, triggers, and hammers designed to fit the needs of that hypothetical person, the average man. They are supposed to fit the hand of a five-foot-two-inch, one-hundred-and-fifty pounder as well as they fit the hand of a six-foot-four-inch, two-hundred-and-fifty pounder. The fact that it is possible for all sizes, shapes and descriptions of men even to fire the gun is a credit to the ingenuity of the handgun designers.

If you are carrying a handgun for legitimate defensive purposes, it is your obligation to be able to use the gun effectively. For this reason you must be sure that the firearm is altered to fit your hand correctly. Few shooters realize how many aids are available to them, aids that may improve their shooting by 50 to 100 per cent or more. Most shooters are ignorant of the work that gunsmiths and others have done in designing these aids.

I remember the police officer who, some time ago, began dropping around the shop. Although he was extremely fond of guns and shooting, he shamefacedly admitted that the best he could shoot was about 65 out of a possible 100 on the standard police target at twenty yards. Constant practice hadn't done much to increase his marksmanship either. His service revolver was a Colt Official Police Revolver with a four-inch barrel, which in my opinion is the finest service revolver made.

I asked him to aim and dry-fire the gun a few times and watched him closely. He showed almost every shooting fault in the book. He needed a much larger grip on the gun than the standard stock that he had. His index finger looped in the trigger well in toward the second joint. The action of

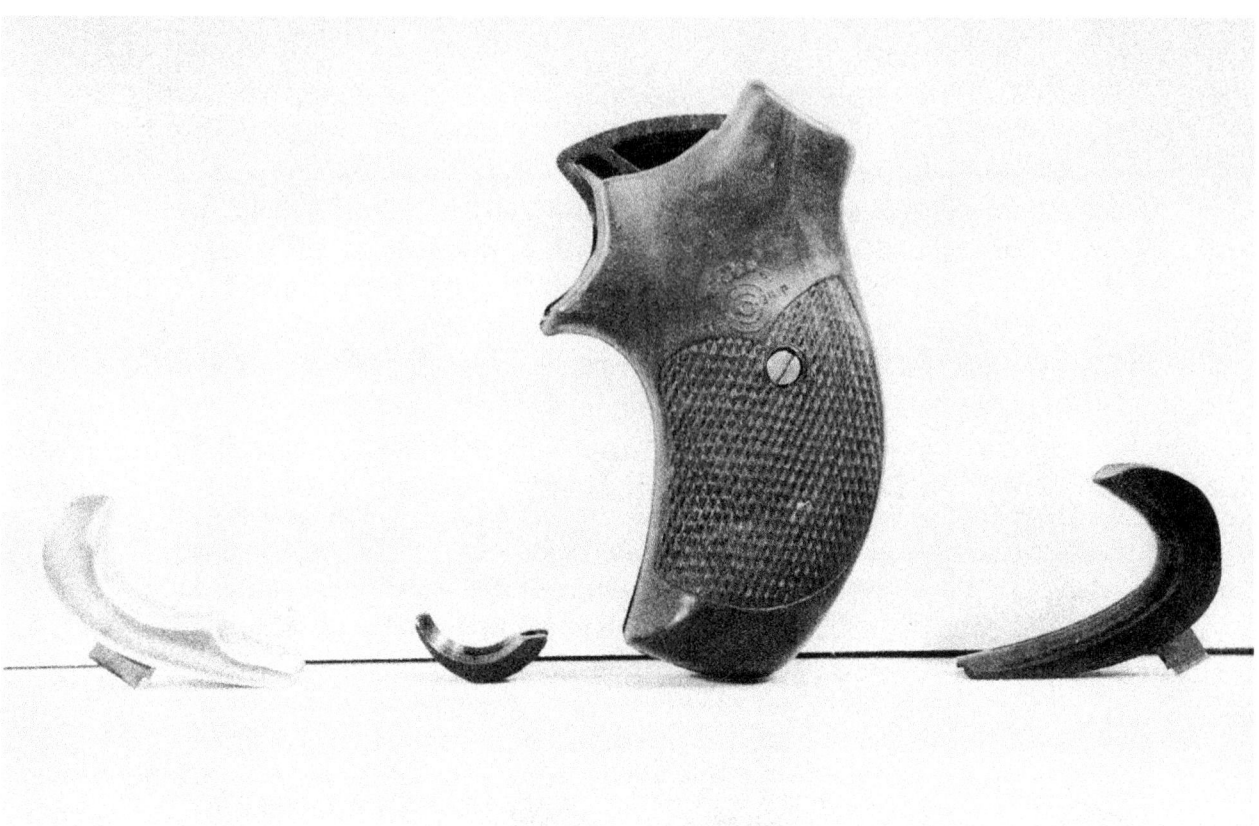

(Left to right) Tyler T-grip, Flaig Ace trigger shoe, Fitz Gunfighter grip, Mershon grip adapter.

his revolver was not so crisp and free of "creep" as it should have been, a fault common with all mass-produced guns.

I suggested that he buy the Colt target stocks of the type used on the .357, that he get the target hammer used on the Officers' Model Match, and that he invest a couple of dollars in trigger shoes. I insisted he get the action of his revolver honed and polished, and the sights checked and corrected.

After he had done all this, he shot a neat 96 out of a possible 100. Thus, by adapting his gun, his score was boosted by 31 points, under the same conditions and with no additional practice. Now this avid powder-burner consistently averages better than 98 points. And he does this excellent shooting with a service weapon, not a target pistol.

There are three outstanding examples of guns whose grips are so cleverly designed that they seem to make any changes unnecessary. These three masterpieces of gun design are the Colt Single-Action Army Model (otherwise known as the Frontier Six-Shooter), the Luger Parabellum semi-automatic pistol of World War I fame, and the recently designed Hi-Standard .22 revolver.

These three guns can be shot effectively by almost everyone without

3 masterpieces of grip design

(Top to bottom)

Ruger Single Six

Luger Parabellum semi-automatic

Hi-Standard .22 Sentinel

the need for changes or alterations. The grip of the Hi-Standard Sentinel, designed by Harry Seifried, is such a beautiful job that it seems a shame to waste it on a gun of only .22 caliber.

GRIP ADAPTERS

There are many custom grip makers who specialize in making your gun fit your hand properly. One of the most skillful of all grip makers was the late Lew Sanderson of Detroit. Herrett also makes a fine line of custom stocks, especially their Detective Series stocks.

One objection to them is the sharp edge at the base of the butt, and the fact that the surfaces are checkered instead of smooth. Grips on guns that have to be carried in concealment should have rounded edges and smooth surfaces, so as not to wear the clothing. If you insist on having checkered grips, sandpaper the sharp edges and save your clothing.

Rounded grips also save split seconds of time in drawing and firing the weapon. There is no involuntary hesitation when your hand slams the rounded edges of the pistol grip.

The standard pistol grip can be easily altered to fit your personal needs by the use of a grip adapter. The Packmeyer and Mershon grip adapters have long been favorites of many peace officers. I prefer the Tyler T adapter for my own use.

The correct way to determine the size adapter your hand requires is to take the best and most comfortable hold possible on the weapon. You should grip the gun so that the barrel feels like an extension in a line parallel to your hand, wrist, and forearm. The backstrap of the weapon should be centered in the webbing between your thumb and forefinger. Note carefully the space between your second finger and the portion of the frame extending between your thumb and forefinger. Then check the space between your second finger and the section of the frame between the grip and the trigger guard. The adapter you use should fill the space snugly — nothing less and nothing more.

TRIGGER SHOES

After you have fitted your gunstock properly, rapidly draw and dry-fire the weapon a number of times. Each time, note the position of your forefinger on the trigger. If your trigger finger always presses the trigger with the ball at the point between the first joint and the tip of the finger, your gun now fits your hand.

However, if your finger wraps around the trigger, exerting pressure at the first joint, or between the first and second joints, as is usually the case with persons having medium or large hands, you should put trigger shoes on your gun. If you consistently shoot to the left of your point of aim, you need trigger shoes. Smith & Wesson, realizing this, has recently made available special wide-groove target triggers for use on their "K"-frame revolvers and also on their heavy-frame target revolvers and Magnums. Trigger shoes are one of the greatest boons ever invented for the handgun shooter. They can cure more shooting faults than months on the practice range.

HAMMERS

The third step in fitting the gun to your hand is the selection of the proper hammer. Sight your gun on an object and then cock it, still keeping the object in your sights. If you are able to do this successfully, the hammer of your gun is right for you. If, however, the act of cocking the weapon throws your sights too far off the point of aim, you should change the hammer for one more suited to your requirements.

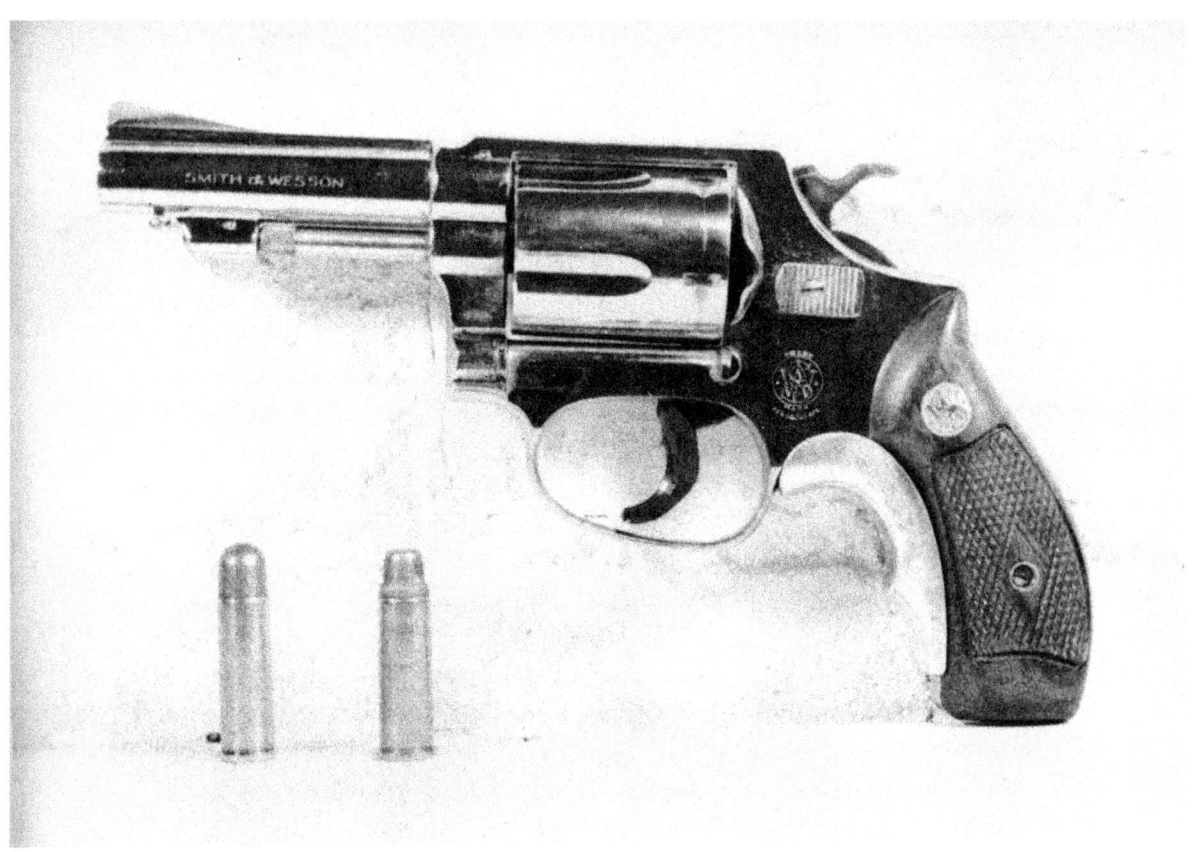

Smith & Wesson .38 Chief Special 3" barrel with Tyler T-grip adapter and Ace trigger shoe.

Although the standard hammer used on Colt police revolvers is not too bad, the Colt target hammer, as used on the Officer's Model Match, will greatly improve the efficiency of the Colt Marshal, Official Police, and Trooper revolvers. The standard hammer on the Smith & Wesson Military Police is very difficult for most people to cock. However, their target hammer, which will fit that gun, is the best hammer sold commercially. It can be used to excellent advantage on any of their K-frame series.

Why manufacturers put fine hammers on target revolvers, which are used only to punch holes in paper, while they put any hammer available on a gun used to defend your life, has always been a source of wonder to me. Some time ago a police officer from one of New York's rougher precincts came to see me. He had just been involved in a gun fight in which, while shooting at a stolen car, he missed his target completely and wounded an innocent bystander. He'd been cleared by the judge, but shocked at what had happened, he was now coming to me for help in making himself an effective combat shooter. I advised him to adapt the gun to fit his hand, which was very heavy. He did so, putting on trigger shoes, target hammer, and grip adapter. His score improved immediately.

A short time later this officer was involved in another shooting. Once again he stood in front of the same judge who had heard the evidence before. The difference was that in the second case he neatly dispatched a holdup man with one bullet in a running gun fight.

The judge's only comment, upon recognizing him, was "Your shooting has improved!"

For some reason known only to themselves, Smith & Wesson have discontinued making their famous humpback hammer, a design preferred by many experts through the years. Herrett manufactures an off-side hammer "shoe" that can be fitted to the hammer of most standard revolvers. I recommend its use when wide-spur target hammers are not available for your shooting iron.

SIGHTS

Many shooters consider the standard sights on their handguns to be quite satisfactory. Actually, they are anything but adequate for a person carrying a gun for defensive purposes. Eighty per cent of all gun fights occur after dark. If you can see blue-steel sights on a dimly lit street, you're a better man than I am! It is possible to see the sights on a nickel-plated gun under these conditions, but the flash of the nickel on the gun can also betray your position to your adversary. A solid-gold block, set just below the uppermost tip of your front sight, is one of the best answers to this problem. It will catch and reflect all available light. A gold-bead post sight is effective for this purpose, but such sights have a tendency to hang up inside a holster and slow your draw in an emergency.

For this reason — this hang-up in the holster — I recommend the gold block, inlaid into the standard sight. Placing it below the tip of the sight insures greater accuracy in the dark, since the tendency of most shooters is to take too much sight in night shooting.

I cannot recommend the use of adjustable sights on a service or defensive weapon. Target sights are of great value on the target range, the purpose for which they were intended. On a service revolver, which gets banged around in constant daily use, adjustable sights get knocked out of line. In this shape they aren't much better than having no sights at all. I feel that a gun manufacturer would do well to improve the sight picture of the fixed type used on the service weapon. Colt has recently improved the sights on its Detective Special, Cobra, Agent, and Police Positive Special revolvers, but greater depth as well as greater width of the sight picture would be of even greater value to the combat shooter.

Manufacturers today don't take the care they should in zeroing in the

Colt Detective Special with inlaid gold block in front sight. It has redheaded screws set on either side of the sight. The device, invented by Ed Wallace, is excellent for fast sighting in combat use.

sights. Invariably the gun shoots high, low, or to one side. You would do well to seek the help of a competent gunsmith, who has range facilities to check your sights.

Holdout revolvers having two-inch barrels invariably shoot high above the point of aim. The western Super Police ammunition with a 200-grain bullet will drop in flight and compensate for this inaccuracy. These 200-grain bullets must be used only with the Detective Special and Chief Special, regular weight. The heavier bullet is also more effective in combat. This ammunition should not be used in any air-weight revolvers because it puts too much strain on the light guns.

A Secret Service man, who was assigned to a White House detail, came into my shop a few years ago. His gun was one of the best examples of adapting the weapon to special needs that I have ever seen. In a gunfight with a counterfeiting gang, before his present assignment, he had carried a snub-nose .38 special. In the heat of the gun fight he discovered that his bullets were not penetrating the automobile, only a short distance away, from which his foe was returning his fire. His partner, who was shooting the same ammunition from a regulation service revolver, drilled through the car and nailed the culprit.

There is nothing like a gun fight to make a true believer! This man was no exception. He bought a custom Smith & Wesson .357 Magnum with honed action. The gun had a four-inch barrel equipped with a King Ramp Reflector front sight and a police night sight, by the same makers, as a rear sight. He completed the job with a Mershon ten-point grip and Ace trigger shoes.

His reason for having such an efficient gun was simply that he did not know under what conditions someone might make a try for the President's life. He wanted a gun of a caliber heavy enough to be effective both at short range and added distance. His special sights were such that under almost any light conditions he could shoot effectively. I tested the sights in a dim basement. With the light from just one small window I was able to line them up with perfect ease. It is comforting to know that our President is protected so effectively.

Some gun cranks can't seem to let well enough alone and go overboard in trying to adapt the gun to their needs. The most common mutilations are dehorning the hammer spur and cutting away the front of the trigger guard. In appearance, this looks just dandy; in practice, it leaves much to be desired. The mutilated hammer precludes any single-action shooting in a gun fight but I'll defy them to hit a running man at 150 yards with these monstrosities. They may be all right for an affair of honor in a phone booth or a small closet, but there are times when a handgun is called upon to perform with an accuracy approaching that of a rifle. At such times careful and deliberate single-action shooting is the only answer.

As for removing the front part of the trigger guard, anyone who does that is a prize optimist. A trigger guard, as its name implies, was put on the gun to guard the trigger; to prevent its being snagged on a door handle of a car, in thick brush, or by a wild swing in a hand-to-hand tussle. A gun with a mutilated trigger guard can be put out of commission if it is dropped, or if it's used to belt somebody over the head. All air-weight guns and one standard-weight revolver made of inferior steel, are notoriously apt to become inoperable if dropped or used as a club.

Cutting the trigger guard is alleged to make for "faster" shooting. The fastest men I have ever seen have kept their trigger guards intact. I have found a standard trigger guard no hazard in quick-draw shooting, but I have experienced a decided tendency of the trigger finger to hang up on the tip of the mutilated guard on the second or third squeeze during a rapid-fire burst of double-action shooting. These wounded "animals" make interesting conversation pieces but I'd hate to stake my life on them when the chips are down.

Some men with very large fingers do have trouble getting their finger in the trigger guard with speed. It is possible to remove about half of the steel from the front of the guard, on the right side of the guard for right-handed shooters. The guard remains intact, but extra room is allowed for speedier entry of the finger.

CONCEALMENT BUTTS

One form of "mutilation" that I do favor is the reshaping of the butt on many of the guns in use today, when they are to be carried in concealment. The best grip designed for concealment use was that of the old Colt "Double Action Lightning." This bird's-head or Derringer-type grip is superior to the rounded butt and cut-down stocks on the holdout guns available today. The butts on today's holdout revolvers are either so small that it's impossible to get a good shooting grip on them in a hurry or so large that they're not readily concealable. The bird's-head grip is the logical compromise between the two. It affords enough grip to grab and hold onto in a hurry, and yet it has no sharp edges or protruding corners to betray its presence when carried in concealment.

Many different materials are used in making grips, not all of them satisfactory. Plastic grips are too light and they often warp. Stag is good when the gun is worn exposed, but tends to wear the clothing when the weapon is carried in concealment. Pearl handles, so dear to the hearts of rookies, tend to be slippery and to break if the gun is dropped. Bone, horn, wood, and ivory are excellent. You can shape the wooden stocks that come on your gun quite easily. If you sandpaper off the checkering, and round off the bottom, you will have an excellent concealment grip.

ACTIONS AND TRIGGER PULL

It is a common misconception that trigger pulls should be fitted to individual tastes. The practice of lightening the pull to hair-trigger proportions is dangerous for two reasons. First, it increases the hazard of accidental or premature discharge. Second, since there is a variance of 100 per cent on the thickness of metal on the primers in standard factory loads, a too-light spring tension frequently results in hung fire.

True, the standard assembly-line action leaves a great deal to be desired. The best way to test a new weapon for smoothness of action is to dry-fire it, double-action, very slowly. This will show up the rough spots in the action. Since the lightest trigger pull that is safe on the gun, under all conditions, is a two-and-a-half pound one, the remedy for harsh, creepy action is to have it honed and polished by an expert gunsmith.

In a gun that has short action, it is not advisable to tamper with the trigger pull at all. The short distance the hammer has to fall necessitates the greater force behind it to be sure of igniting the cartridge. If you have a honed action and trigger shoes, the effect will be the feel of a hair-trigger job with safety from accidental discharge.

Any regular action, when all the parts have been honed and polished, can be made so smooth that you feel it was set in ice. A really good job takes many hours of labor, a rather expensive proposition that should be undertaken only by a very competent gunsmith. Nevertheless the best action I have ever seen was on a Colt Detective Special belonging to a New York State policeman who had spent months smoothing and polishing the action himself.

Two of the best gunsmiths on revolver actions in the country are George Hyde, at 552 Third Street, Brooklyn, and "Goody" Goodhue, at the Colt Factory in Hartford, Connecticut. They are responsible for some of the finest actions in existence.

For any work requiring the services of a gunsmith, you should make sure that the man is qualified to do an expert job. Today there are only a handful of really fine gunsmiths left. Put your gun in their hands, not in those of some half-trained gun butcher. Unfortunately, the fine ones are far outnumbered by the "butchers." To avoid the latter and locate the former is an arduous task, but it will reward you a hundredfold.

Whether you are using it in defense of your life or just for plinking at small game and tin cans, your gun, correctly fitted, can make you the handgunner you want to be.

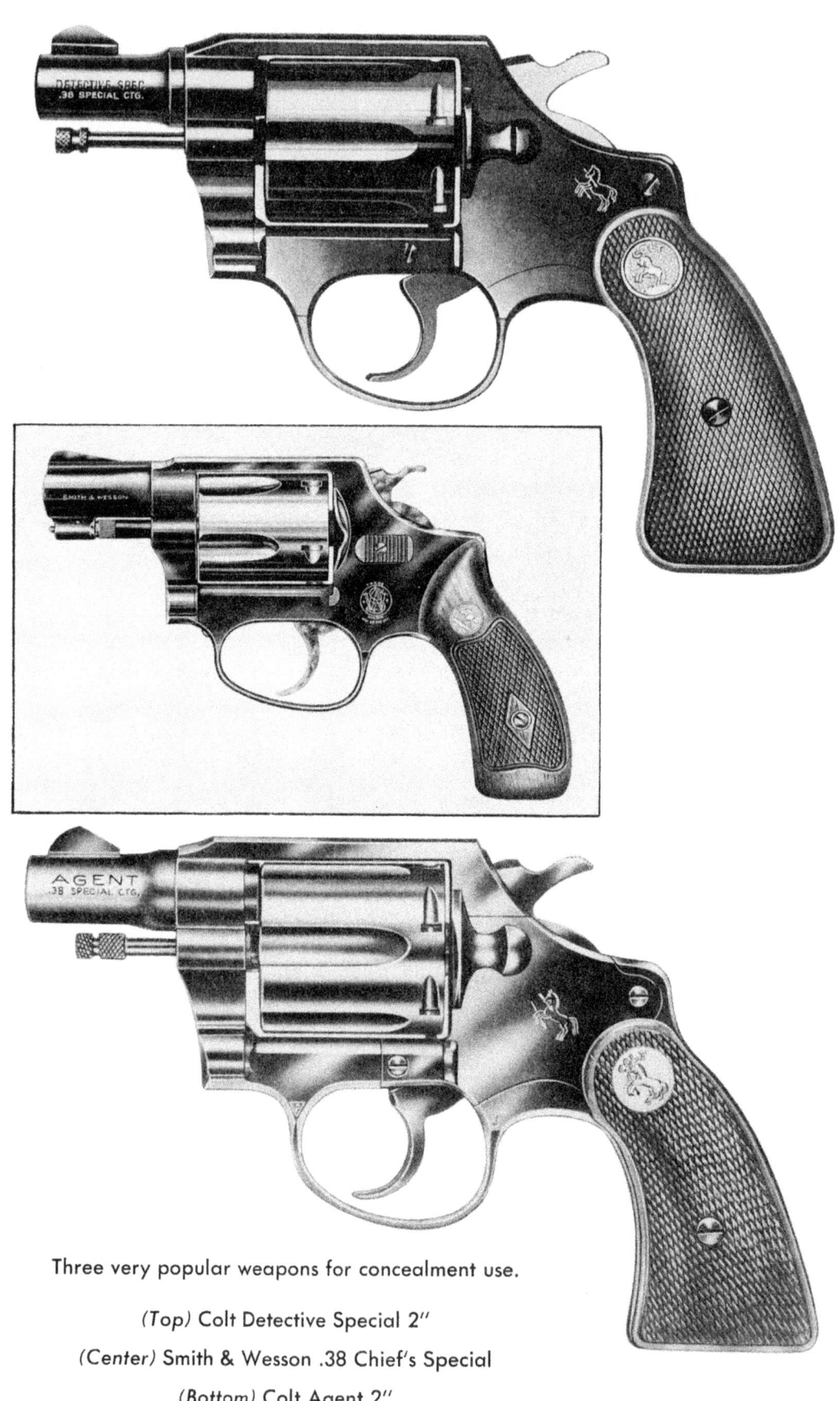

Three very popular weapons for concealment use.

(Top) Colt Detective Special 2"
(Center) Smith & Wesson .38 Chief's Special
(Bottom) Colt Agent 2"

CHAPTER 2

Weapons for Concealment

HANDGUNS for concealment can be divided into two categories, the "carry gun" used by off-duty police officers, detectives, and plain-clothesmen; and the "holdout" used by undercover men or, as a secondary emergency weapon, by police officers desiring the insurance of a second gun. No carry gun should be of less than .38 caliber. A .38 Special caliber is even more desirable. When choosing a carry gun, get a regular-weight, all-steel gun whenever possible. The air-weight guns with aluminum or magnesium alloy frames, which have been enjoying an undeserved popularity in recent years, do not, in my opinion, fill the needs of a handgun. This type of weapon, sadly deficient in strength and ruggedness, will not stand up under heavy loads. If fired often enough to insure an adequate degree of marksmanship with the weapon, they shoot loose. The screws loosen up in the softer metal. They also are inclined to become inoperable if they are dropped, and heaven help you if you have to hit anybody over the head with one — the human head will prove tougher every time. As a matter of fact, Colt's regular-weight revolvers are the only handguns that seem to be able to stand up under such punishment. This fact simply should not be discounted; you'd be amazed at how often a felon is subdued by having a pistol barrel bent over his dome. Wyatt Earp may or may not have been the first peace officer to use this method, but he was far from being the last. I know of one detective in a fairly active precinct who put so many revolvers out of commission in tussles with felons that he finally solved the problem by carrying a Colt

New Service .45 with cut-down barrel and grips. The mere appearance of this in his hand proved enough to cow the most ardent cop fighter.

In the standard-weight carry guns the Smith & Wesson .38-caliber Terrier is the smallest gun to be carried with any degree of safety. It is effective only when loaded with cartridges having semi-wad-cutter bullets of not less than 180 grains. The Smith & Wesson Chief Special with two-inch barrel and the Colt's Detective Special are reasonably effective at close range when loaded with the Western .38 Super Police cartridges having blunt-nosed 200-grain bullets. The Smith & Wesson Chief Special with the three-inch barrel is the best and most effective carry gun available "as is" from the factory. It is nearly as effective as the regular .38 Special Service revolvers.

The best of all carry guns, however, is a Colt Police Positive Special with the barrel shortened to three inches and the butt bird's-headed. This gun is small enough to fit comfortably in a pocket holster, yet it has the six-shot .38 Special caliber with ballistics characteristics only slightly less effective than the famous Colt Official Police revolver.

In my opinion, it is desirable for a carry gun to be either nickel- or chrome-plated. These guns by their very nature are designed to be worn in concealment holsters that hold them close to the body, and so they are extremely vulnerable to rust induced by perspiration. A plated gun, given reasonable care, is not affected by moisture to anywhere near the same degree. A plated gun wiped clean every day or so with a piece of Kleenex tissue will remain in perfect condition for many years.

There is a popular misconception that the shorter the barrel of the gun, the easier it may be carried in concealment. This is just not true. A small-

Smith & Wesson Chief Special .38 3″ barrel with Fitz Gunfighter grip and Ace trigger shoe. The extra one inch of barrel provides sufficiently increased bore capacity to make this one of the most compact, hard-hitting concealment guns available. *(Right)* **Smith & Wesson Chief Special 3″ barrel worn on the right hip in a tight-fitting scabbard.**

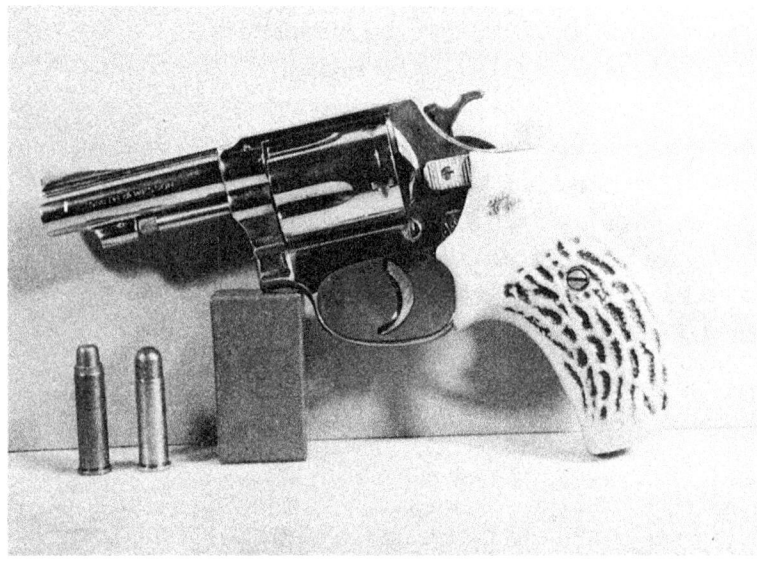
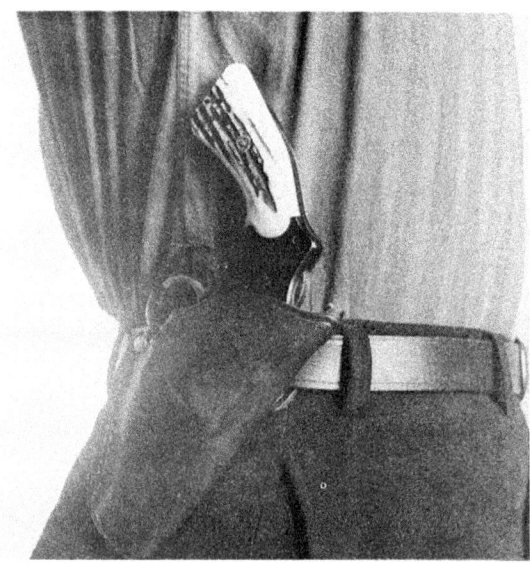

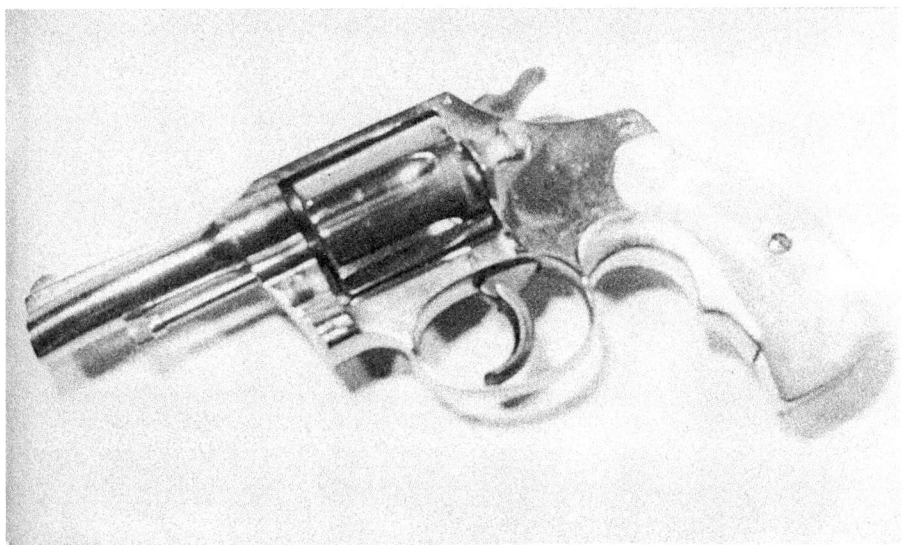
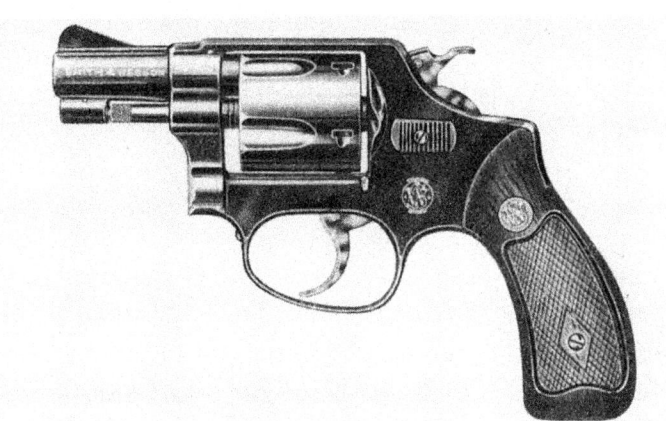
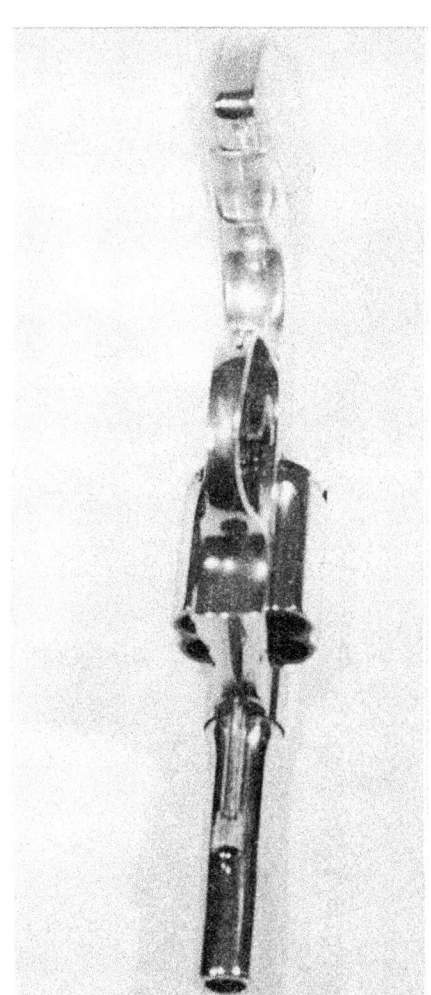

Chic Gaylord's Metropolitan Special Adaptation of the Police Positive Special. The Metropolitan Special was designed as the perfect defense weapon for concealment use.

(Left) Barrel cut to 3"
    Ramp front sight
    Butt bird's-headed
    Tyler T-grip adapter
    Ace Trigger shoes

(Right) Relieved trigger guard
    Robert Frielich, Gunsmith

(Bottom) The Smith & Wesson Terrier — a popular concealment weapon that is also widely used by policemen.

framed gun, such as the Terrier, Chief Special, or Detective Special, with a two-inch barrel, can be fairly well concealed in a jacket or pants pocket. However, when carried in a holster, this is not necessarily true. In a holster, the three-inch Chief Special hugs the body far more effectively than does the two-inch Chief in the same type of holster. Colt's Police Positive Special with the four-inch barrel holsters far better than its two-inch counterpart, the Detective Special. The three hardest guns to holster with any degree of comfort and concealment — what I call the "topheavy trio" — are the two-

(Top) Walther PP.
(Bottom) Walther PPK.

inch, Colt Marshal, Smith & Wesson's two-inch Military and Police revolver, and Smith & Wesson's .357 Magnum with the three-and-a-half-inch barrel. These guns have large grips, heavy cylinders and frames, and nowhere near enough barrel to balance them in the holster. Why anyone would carry around so much excess weight in a weapon having such ineffective ballistics is beyond me. Two more inches added to the barrel would increase the total weight of the gun by not over four ounces, resulting in an effective weapon that could be carried with far greater comfort and concealment. One of the most effective carry guns that I have ever seen is the Webley & Scott .455-caliber Irish Constabulary model. This British handgun is not much larger than Colt's Detective Special, yet it packs a wallop like Ingo Johannson's.

I cannot recommend any semi-automatic pistol as a carry gun. The Government Model Colt .45 ACP has the necessary knockdown power but it is a little too heavy and bulky for this purpose. All other smaller automatics lack both dependability and authority because of their jacketed ammunition. If you are an expert enough marksman to call your shots under any and all circumstances, the Walther PP chambered for the .22 long rifle and loaded with Western Super X high-speed hollow-point cartridges can be just about as deadly a weapon as could be desired. It inflicts a much nastier wound than does the standard .38 Special, but it does lack the authority of instant knockdown power, and for that reason it is a risky personal defense gun — except, as I say, in the hands of an expert.

Since the early days of the Western Frontier, many peace officers have liked to carry a holdout or hide-out gun. Two favorites of those old days were the Colt Single Shot and the Remington double-barrel Derringer pistol. These ineffective little weapons were made primarily to shoot across a poker table and the greatest danger was that of blood poisoning resulting from the germ-laden grease coating of the bullet. A single flesh wound was just about as dangerous as a direct hit.

Hide-out weapons have not improved greatly over the years. Various manufacturers have brought out copies of the time-honored Remington Derringer in calibers producing pressures far greater than that fragile frame was ever designed to take. The little German .22-caliber imports are the one exception. Otherwise, there is a definite need for a modern hide-out gun of reasonable power and effectiveness.

I have seen many hide-out guns made by cutting down various light-framed revolvers, usually of the top break "suicide special" design. The best of these weapons are of either the Smith & Wesson .38 caliber or Iver Johnson chambered for Colt's Police Positive .38 shorts. Most of these light-framed revolvers have rather small grips, a desirable feature for a gun of this type. Some of these guns are of the hammerless type. These "lemon-squeezers" can be fired only double action. Others are of the exposed-hammer type. When searching for one of these pistols to adapt for hide-out use, it is best to stick to the known makes of guns such as Smith & Wesson and Iver Johnson. Most of these guns are from thirty to fifty years old, and *nothing older than that should be considered.* Many "Fourth-of-July" guns formerly made in this style would be very dangerous to try to use with today's powerful ammunition.

Many peace officers engaged in undercover work are forced to rely on the midget .25-caliber automatics that are available today. Contrary to general opinion, the same size gun chambered for the .22 short is far more effective than the .25-caliber automatics. We made some tests with two small automatics, one .25-caliber and the other .22 short, and a German .22-caliber over-and-under copy of the Remington double-barreled Derringer. We fired the guns at one-yard range, these guns being intended only for very close work. We fired into a 2,008-page, two-and-a-half-inch thick Manhattan classified telephone book, which we had soaked in water to bring it to a consistency resembling that of human flesh. The bullets from the .25-caliber automatic, a Colt-Astra Cub, penetrated three quarters of an inch and the only deforming of the jacketed bullet was an almost imperceptible flattening of its point. The base was not deformed in any way and slipped readily into the empty case from which it had been fired. The .22 automatic, loaded with Western Super-X hollow-point short cartridges, fired through 2,000 pages before it stopped, just short of complete penetration of the book. The bullets were flattened out, some were split into jagged pieces, and others expanded to a diameter only slightly smaller than that of a .38-caliber bullet. The shots from the double-barreled Derringer, loaded with Western Super-X high-speed Long Rifle hollow-point cartridges, ripped completely through the book, hit the backstop, and ricocheted about one third of the distance back into the book. These bullets were so deformed as to be almost unrecognizable. The hole they made through the wet paper after they had expanded and penetrated about one inch tore a hole that one could put a finger through easily.

This simple test is an acceptable indication of the relative destruction caused by the three different midget weapons. The two automatics were considerably smaller and thus more easily hidden than the Derringer and, in my opinion, if the choice of a hide-out weapon rests between the two small semi-automatic pistols, the pistol chambered for the .22 short would be far more desirable. It has been my experience that by using the proper concealment holsters, today's undercover operative does not have to stake his life on the performance of one of these low-caliber guns. It is possible to conceal the Smith & Wesson Terrier, the Chief Special, or the six-shot Colt Agent in holdout rigs that will enable the wearer to avoid detection.

CHAPTER 3

Personal Defense Weapons

BY FAR the largest segment of the gun-carrying public is composed of police, civilians, and military personnel who carry a weapon in defense of their person, their property, or properties entrusted to them. These people wish to carry their guns in concealment. However, the nature of their work does not require the degree of precision necessary for persons working under cover. The banker, the jeweler, the pay-roll clerk, the doctor and the druggist — in fact, most civilians who, because of their work, find it advisable to carry a gun need a weapon that is reasonably comfortable to carry. Here the gun must be carried on the person in a manner not to attract attention and should be as effective as possible in the unskilled hands of the untrained civilian.

The civilian who carries a firearm should receive marksmanship training from a competent instructor. Too many people — and, unfortunately, this includes large sections of the police and the military — are far from expert in their *handling* of handguns. Before a person is issued a driver's license, he must prove that he is capable of driving a car in a manner that will not be a menace to the lives of others. Permits to carry a pistol are issued all over the country to people who have no more than a vague idea as to which end of the gun the bullet comes out of! Such irresponsible gun toters are a menace to life and property.

The United States Treasury Department's Bureau of Narcotics will not permit one of its agents to carry a gun until he has passed an extremely exacting course of training and is expert in the handling of his weapon. It

Colt Police Positive Special — 4" —
The most practical personal defense weapon for all-around use.

would be wonderful, indeed, if these high standards of the Treasury Department were followed by the military, the police and by law-enforcement agencies that issue pistol permits. Then the innocent bystander would get a much better break than he is getting now.

No one should carry a snub-nosed revolver having a barrel of two inches or less without shooting an average of one hundred rounds a week in practice. Anyone unable to practice his shooting to this extent should carry a gun having a barrel three inches or over, preferably one with a four-inch barrel. In my judgment, Colt's .38 Police Positive Special is the best gun of this type. The Smith & Wesson Chief Special with the three-inch barrel is the smallest acceptable weapon for this use.

Too often a man totally unskilled in the handling of firearms buys a snub-nosed revolver, usually an air-weight model. He does nothing to the gun in the way of adding trigger shoes or special grips or having his action honed. Then, unfortunately, this man is called upon to use his gun in an emergency. Almost certainly he is carrying the gun so that he pulls it in an across-the-body draw. Tense, nervous, and rattled, he begins pulling the trigger almost as soon as the gun clears the holster and doesn't stop pulling it until the gun is empty. If our hero hasn't hit some innocent bystander with the barrage he's laid down, he can consider himself lucky indeed. The felon he was shooting at probably wouldn't have been safer if he'd been in church. If it was a statistically average case he has wounded one or two of those bystanders. Our hero has succeeded in shooting himself into a lot more trouble than he thought he was shooting himself out of! One thing wounded bystanders seem to have in common is that they have a brother-in-law or a close friend who is a practicing attorney, and our boy's misguided missiles

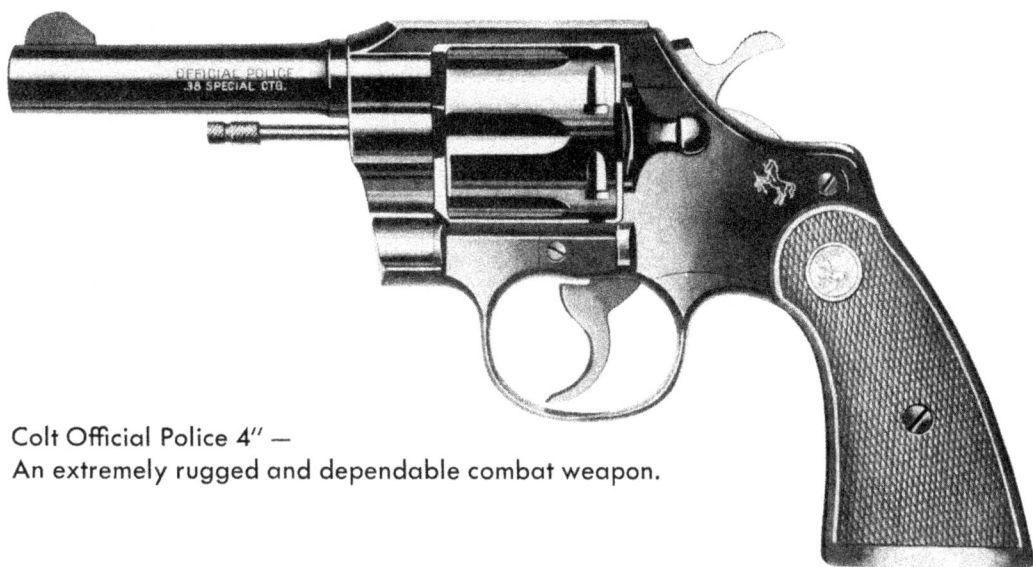

Colt Official Police 4" —
An extremely rugged and dependable combat weapon.

have brought him one or more staggering damage suits. Judges and juries quite rightly take a dim view of having their fellow men shot up for no good reason, and our hero may find himself in hock up to his eyebrows to pay off these claims.

If this poor fellow had bought a gun with a long enough barrel so he could see at a glance in what general direction it was pointed, he would have been much better off to start with. If he had then adapted the gun to fit his hand and spent a little money learning how to shoot, he would have succeeded in giving the "bad guy" his just deserts and would have emerged from the fray a real hero instead of a heel.

As a personal defense weapon, Colt's Official Police with a four-inch barrel is as dependable a gun as you could find. Colt's .357 with the same length barrel is a safe, compact weapon for those desiring still greater performance. No Magnum revolver should be used for work in a city or suburban area: the bullets travel too far and have too great penetration. Most Magnum revolvers have adjustable sights. Such sights are not desirable on a personal defense weapon. Target sights belong on target guns to be used on target ranges. They are too easily knocked out of adjustment in constant holster wear. Smith & Wesson's compact Combat Magnum also has adjustable target sights, although somewhat stronger than the Colt sights. One of the arms companies would do well to produce a rugged, compact .357 having fixed milled sights that would give as clear a sight picture as do the target sights. Colt's Government model .45 ACP can be an effective personal defense pistol when properly holstered. This piece of artillery should not be toted by those who have not mastered it. It is an exceedingly fine gun, however, in the hands of anyone who knows how to shoot it.

Personal Defense Weapons

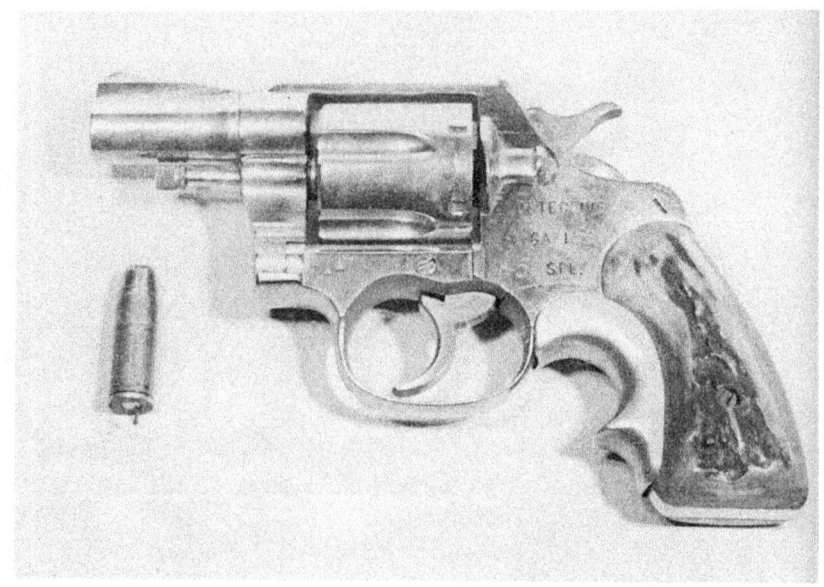

Detective Ganio's .45 Special. This compact "Monster" is a .45 Colt model 1917 revolver with a .45 Colt New Service cylinder and latch. The grip frame has been shortened as has the ejector rod. The barrel has been cut to two-and-one-half inches. A ramp front sight has been added and the rear sight has been built up to provide a target-type sight picture. This deadly weapon fires a "hot" load of ten grains of Unique behind a 280-grain semi-wad-cutter bullet.

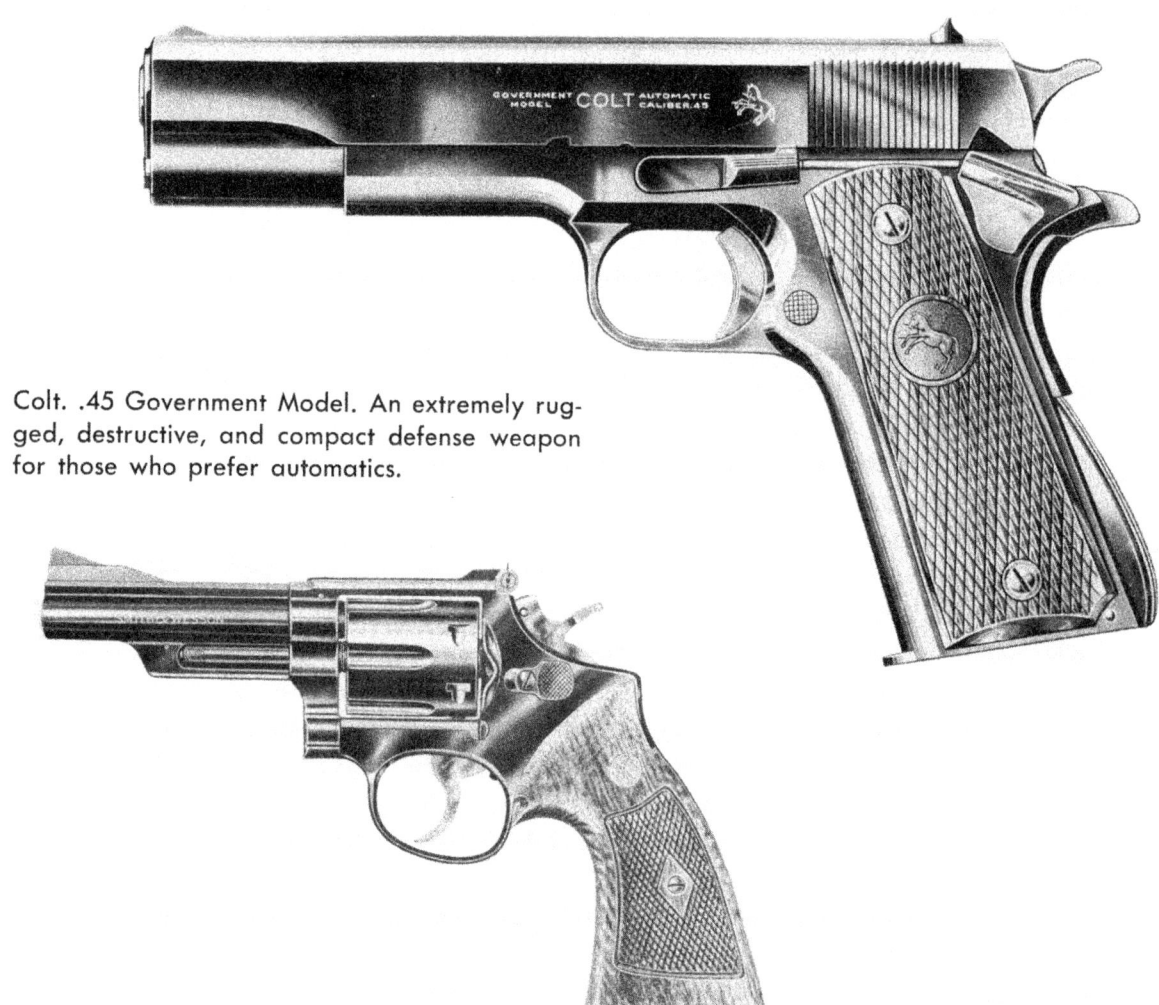

Colt .45 Government Model. An extremely rugged, destructive, and compact defense weapon for those who prefer automatics.

Smith & Wesson .357 Combat Magnum — despite its target sights it is a good personal defense weapon.

CHAPTER 4

Service Weapons

A GOOD SERVICE weapon is one that is so ruggedly constructed that it can take a great deal of rough usage without resultant breakdown or malfunction. It should be sufficiently powerful to knock a man down at seventy-five yards. It must be strong enough so that if it's used as a mace to club a man into submission, such extraordinary use will not produce malfunctions in the weapon. The old Colt New Service .45 with the five-inch barrel was an almost perfect service weapon. If the ejector rod had been enclosed, as Colt now has done in the Python, it would have been unbeatable.

In current production, Smith & Wesson has the 1950 .44 Military as well as the .38-.44 Heavy Duty. These two guns are fundamentally the same except that the .44 has considerably more shocking power. Both of them are heavy-duty service arms, the only ones in their class having milled fixed sights as an integral part of the frame. All of the other heavy-duty revolvers in production today have adjustable sights. They do give a picture far superior to that of most guns having milled sights, but they are apt to be knocked out of alignment by constant holster wear. Such sights are much too easily damaged if the weapon is dropped on a hard or abrasive surface, and sometimes they even drop off and are lost.

Service weapons chambered for the .357 Magnum cartridge should never have less than a six-inch barrel. The type of powder used in the Magnum cartridge necessitates this minimum for any sort of efficiency.

Cartridges of .38 special caliber can be hand-loaded for heavy-duty weapons having barrels under six inches, giving them performance far superior to that of the .357 factory load in the same length barrel. For patrol on the highway and in wide-open areas, extremely long-barreled .357s are ideal. The Smith & Wesson .357 with the eight and three-eighths inch barrel can drive tacks at 200 yards. The Colt Python, in my estimation, has the best balance and smoothest action of any of the .357 service weapons.

The current trend toward reducing the weight and barrel length of magnums seems to me ill-advised. A light gun of heavy caliber has far too much recoil for accuracy. Smith & Wesson's Combat Magnum is the outstanding example of this trend.

Bill Ruger, of the Sturm Ruger Company, is the only manufacturer going in the right direction. He redesigned his .44 Magnum Blackhawk and has now brought it out as the Super Blackhawk with a longer barrel — seven and a half inches — and has added half a pound to the weight of the gun. The new model outperforms his earlier gun and is far more pleasant to shoot. If Smith & Wesson would follow suit and add a pound or two to the meager 47 ounces of their .44 "Mangle-'em" they would have a nice double-action cannon that you *could* shoot double-action.

The Colt Official Police revolver in .38 Special caliber with a four-inch barrel and rounded butt is an ideal service weapon for densely populated metropolitan areas. The Colt Official Police is probably the most famous police service arm in the world. It is rugged, dependable, and thoroughly tested by time. It has good sights and a smooth trouble-free action. This gun can fire high-speed armor-piercing loads. It can safely handle hand loads that would turn its competitors into flying shards of steel. When loaded with the Winchester Western 200-grain Super Police loads, it is an effective man-stopper.

Smith & Wesson .44 Magnum, 6½" barrel.

(Top) Smith & Wesson — 1950 Model Army .45 Caliber. This gun is a favorite with men in service because it is chambered for the .45 ACP cartridge.

(Center) Colt New Service .45 with Mershon grip adapter and Ace trigger shoe. This gun was one of the favorite man stoppers of all times — rugged, dependable and accurate.

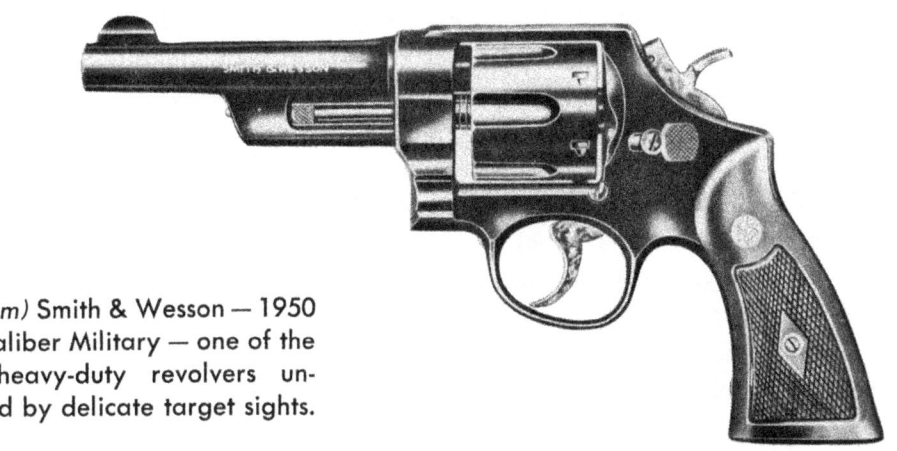

(Bottom) Smith & Wesson — 1950 .44 Caliber Military — one of the few heavy-duty revolvers untainted by delicate target sights.

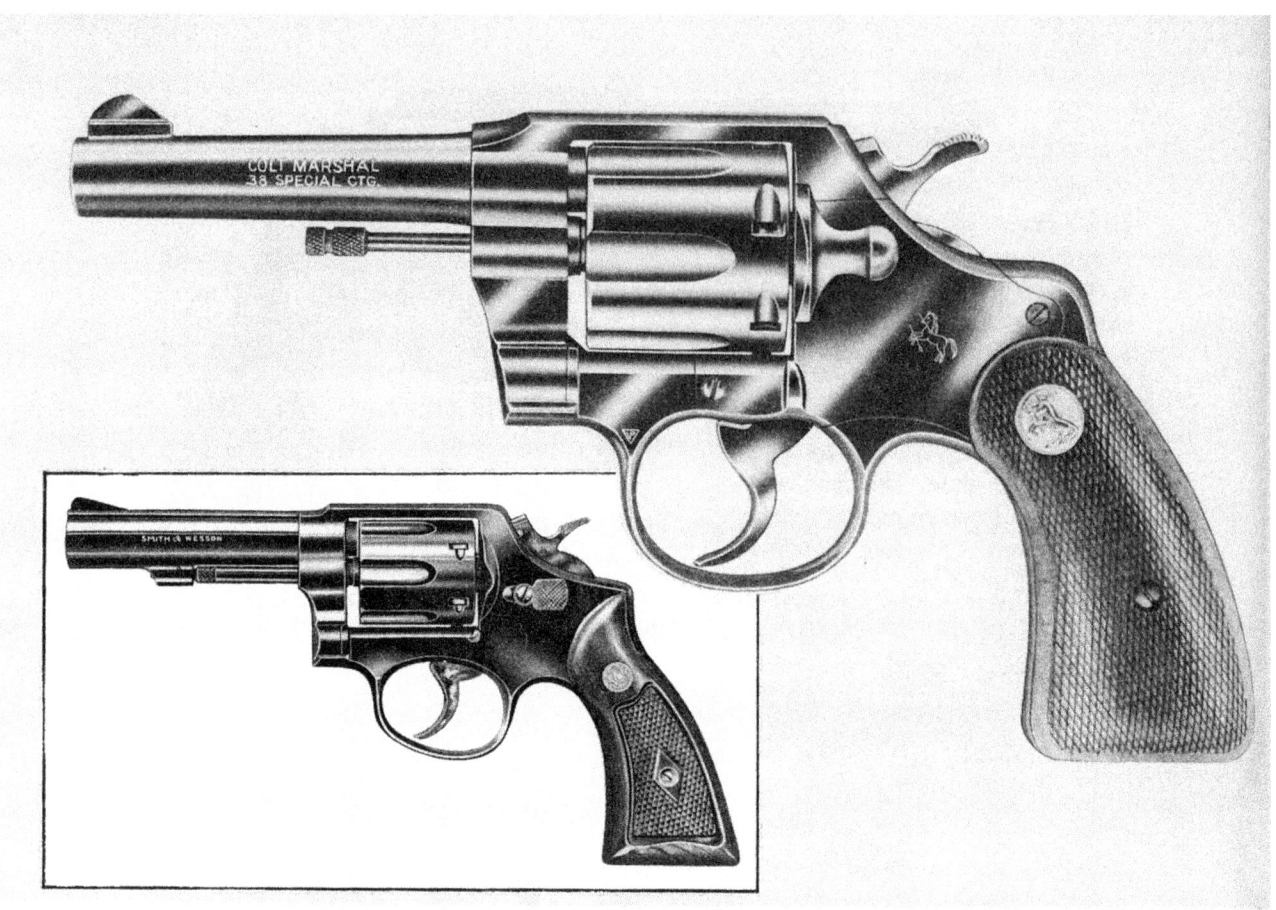

Colt Official Police 4" barrel — round butt. The best designed of the .38 caliber Service weapons — the round butt enables it to be carried both in uniform and plainclothes.

(Insert) Smith & Wesson — Military & Police with heavy barrel. The newest addition to the Smith & Wesson family.

Smith & Wesson is bringing out a redesigned .38-caliber Military and Police that has a heavy stovepipe barrel four inches in length. Douglas Hellstrom of Smith & Wesson assures me that the cylinder is made of a new and stronger steel. The gun has a very nice hang and balance. The sights are far superior to the sights on the current Military and Police. The cut in the cylinder for the cylinder stop is still the thinnest part of the chamber wall. If they would only move that cut over into the thick webbing between the chambers, I'd feel more comfortable about shooting hot loads. However, they do say that the new steel gives the gun sufficient strength to handle high-speed loads successfully.

The Colt .357 with the six-inch barrel is a very good economy-priced .357. It would be better if a little more weight were added to it, by way of a stovepipe barrel, as was done with the Officer's Model Match pistol of a few years back. It would also be better as a service weapon if it had fixed milled sights. My unsolicited advice to Colt is to streamline their New Service revolver and bring it out in .357 Magnum and .44 Magnum.

The caliber that I feel would be the most effective of them all is a .41 Magnum firing a 200-grain semi-wad-cutter bullet at a velocity of about fifteen hundred feet per second. This should be an ideal service load, combining the best features of the .357 and .44 Magnum loads. I have talked with gun manufacturers who liked the idea and saw the merits of the load. I have also talked with ballistics men from a major ammunition company who were enthusiastic over the possibilities of such a new caliber. Maybe some day they'll get together, and the cop will get the benefit of a far more effective service weapon than any available to him today.

(Top) Colt Trooper 4" barrel. *(Bottom)* Colt Official Police. These two service weapons are also made in .22 caliber.

CHAPTER 5

Guns for Combat Practice

Few gun toters are such expert marksmen that there is no room for improvement. The surest way to become an expert shot is through constant practice. Few of us are fortunate enough to have an unlimited supply of ammunition with which to practice. Centerfire ammunition is quite expensive, which tends to limit the amount of practice that we can do. One solution, of course, is to invest in hand-loading equipment and roll your own ammunition. A good set of reloading tools, dies, etc., though calling for a considerable outlay of cash in the beginning, is a very worth-while investment. It will pay for itself in short order through drastically reduced ammunition costs. Many people, however, have neither the time, space, nor inclination to undertake making their own ammunition. The answer is for them to get a .22-caliber gun as close as possible to the centerfire one they are using for personal defense.

If your service weapon is the Colt .38 Official Police revolver you are fortunate, not only because it is an exceptionally fine police weapon, but also because the identical gun is made in .22 caliber. This is also true if your personal defense gun is a Colt. 357, Trooper or Officer's Model Match Target revolver. The .22 Trooper revolver is an excellent double for the .38 Trooper and .357. The Officer's Model Match .22 is a small-bore duplication of the long-barreled .357 and the .38-caliber Officer's Model Match. The K-22 Combat Masterpiece is, as its name implies, the .22-caliber double of the .38 Combat Masterpiece and the .357 Combat Magnum. The Standard

K-22 can serve as stand-in for its brother the K-38. If your Combat gun is a .38 Chief Special or .38 Terrier, then the Smith & Wesson .22-.32 Kit gun is a stop-gap .22 duplicate. Unfortunately, this gun has target sights that do not duplicate the sights on its .38-caliber counterpart. This will make for problems in holstering the gun. However, it is a better practice gun than no gun at all. The Standard .22-.32 Kit gun can, with the same limitations, serve as stand-in for the Smith & Wesson .38 Regulation Police and the .32 hand ejector.

Conversion units of .22-caliber are available for Colt's .45 ACP Government Model semi-automatic pistol and for the Super .38 semi-automatic pistol. There is also a .22-caliber conversion unit manufactured by Erma for the 9-mm. Luger Parabellum semi-automatic pistol. In the matter of hang and balance, the .22-caliber Ruger semi-automatic pistol is a reasonable double for the 9-mm. The High Standard Duramatic is a fine economy-priced stand-in for the Luger. If your service weapon is a Smith & Wesson Military and Police revolver, the best practice stand-in for your weapon is High Standard's .22-caliber Sentinel revolver, which comes in a wide variety of barrel lengths ranging from their snub-nosed model, with two-and-three-eighths inch barrel, through a three-inch barrel, a four-inch barrel, and a six-inch barrel. Dollar for dollar, I think this little gun gives you more gun for your money than any other handgun sold in America today.

After a little action work that I did myself in less than half an hour (I work over the actions of all my guns) the Hi-Standard Sentinel revolvers that I own have resulted in a bunch of smooth little nine-shooters that outperform guns costing twice their price. My favorite quick-draw gun is a nickel-plated snub-nose with a double-action hammer. After polishing the action, and removing the single-action notch from the trigger and shortening the hammer throw to seven eighths of an inch, rounding off the sharp corners on the front sight, and adding trigger shoes and Mershon grip adapter, I have a little gem of speed with which I draw and fire in less than a tenth of a second. Measured by an electronic timer, before a TV studio audience, I drew and fired in four one-hundredths of a second. I cannot be too strong in my endorsement of the Hi-Standard Sentinel revolver. It provides the most economical means of practice for combat shooting available today. The low price tag on the gun and the economy of the .22 loads enable the peace officer to enjoy vitally necessary practice at the lowest possible cost.

If your personal defense weapon is a Colt or Ruger single-action revolver, the best stand-in for your six-shooter is Ruger's single-action .22 Single-six in the all-steel model. This is a well-made, well-balanced, small-

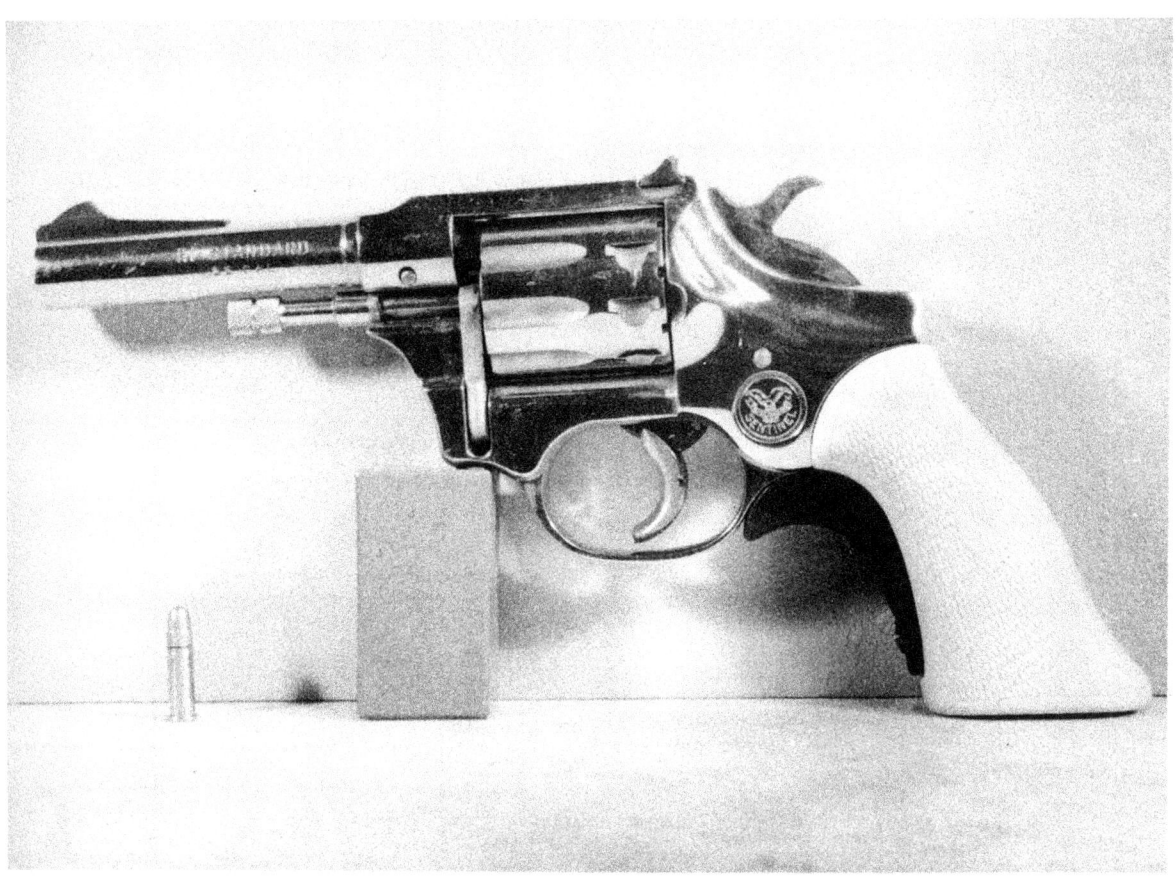

Hi-Standard Sentinel 4" barrel with Mershon grip adapter, honed action and smoothed trigger shoes. An ideal gun for fast-draw combat practice.

bore single-action. The grip, trigger, and hammer action closely approximate that of its heavy-caliber big brother's; in my opinion, it is the best of the single-action .22's. The Ruger single-six air-weight .22 and Colt's Frontier Scout do not have the hang and balance of the large-caliber single action, and, therefore, leave much to be desired in combat practice.

Both the Iver Johnson and Harrington & Richardson top-break revolvers in the .38 Smith & Wesson caliber have their counterpart in the .22-caliber guns of the same make and model. These Harrington & Richardson and Iver Johnson .22's can also serve as doubles for the Webley & Scott .38. Since the only way to become a good shot is through plenty of shooting, these .22-caliber counterparts will greatly increase your skill and efficiency with the heavy-caliber guns.

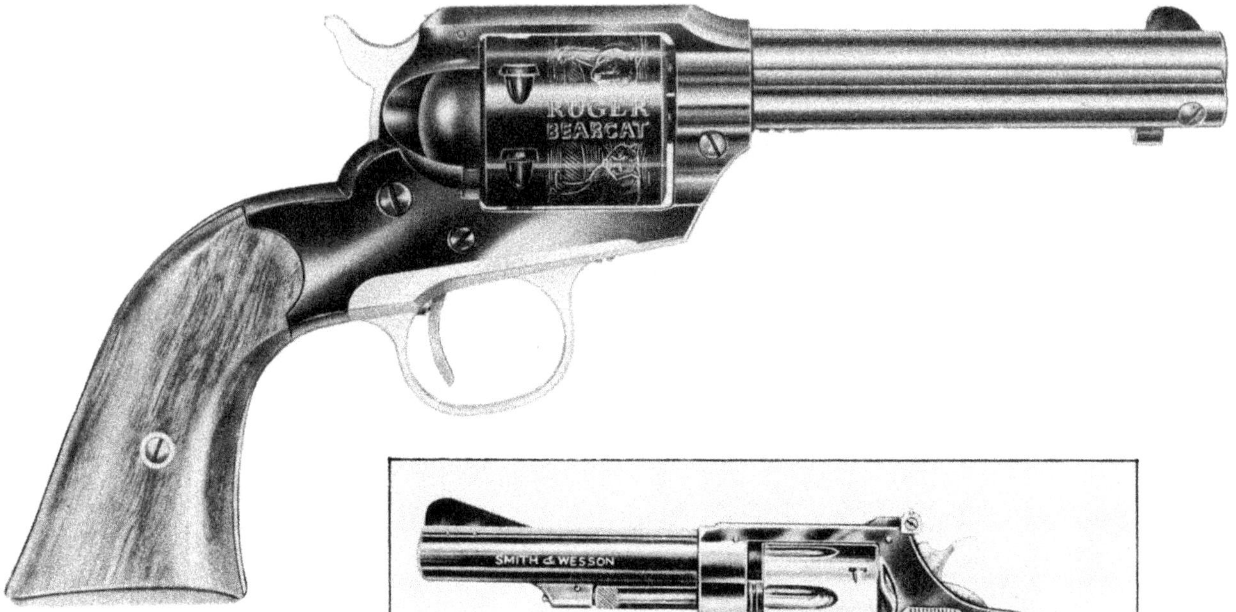

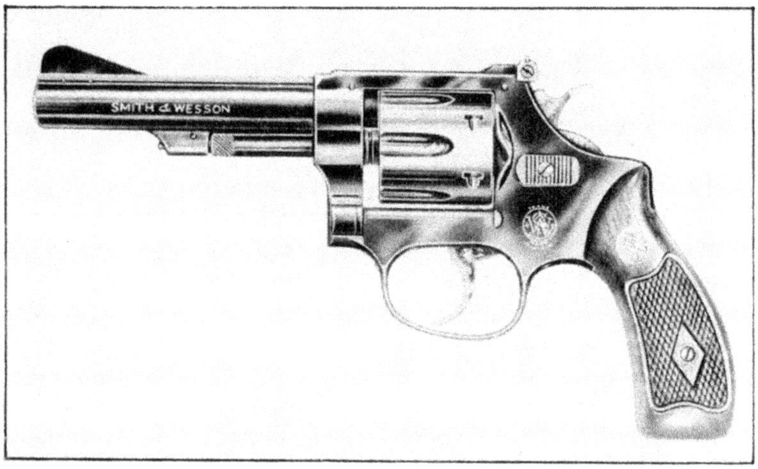

(Top) Ruger Bearcat.

(Bottom) Ruger Single Six — 5½" barrel.

(Insert) Smith & Wesson .22-.32 Kit Gun, 4" barrel, all steel. The finest fun gun available today.

CHAPTER 6

The Fun Guns

THE FUN GUN, as its name implies, is a gun whose primary function is to provide pleasure, relaxation, and pure enjoyment to its user. It is not primarily intended for the protection of life and property, nor is it necessarily as accurate as the super-grade precision target handgun, nor is it a game killer without peer. Yet it may possess many of the properties of these other guns. The fun gun is made for the largest and most enthusiastic segment of the shooting public, the plinkers. The pistol plinker, as a rule, has graduated from rifle plinking. Through pistol plinking he will discover the phase of handgun shooting that interests him most. He will probably go on to spend more of his time developing that phase of shooting, but chances are he never will forsake completely his first love, plinking.

I'm not going out on much of a limb when I say the finest fun gun available today is Smith & Wesson's all-steel .22-.32 Kit Gun with a four-inch barrel. When fitted with Fitz Gun Fighter Grips, or Herrett's Detective Series Grips, and equipped with Flaig's Ace Trigger Shoe, it is well-nigh a perfect companion on a hike or a hunt, or just for plinking at tin cans in the back yard.

If you're intrigued with the romance of the Old West and no gun feels like a gun unless it has the hang of a single-action, Ruger's all-steel Single-six is the ideal six-gun for you, when you're reliving the *High Noon* bit or blazing away at a paper picnic plate. Ruger's newcomer, the Bearcat, will, I predict, soon become one of the most popular fun guns in the country: It's

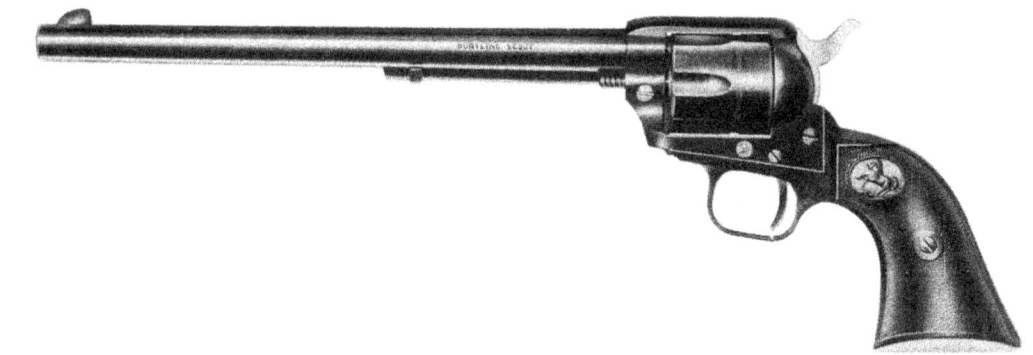

The Colt Buntline Scout — an exceptionally accurate .22 plinker.

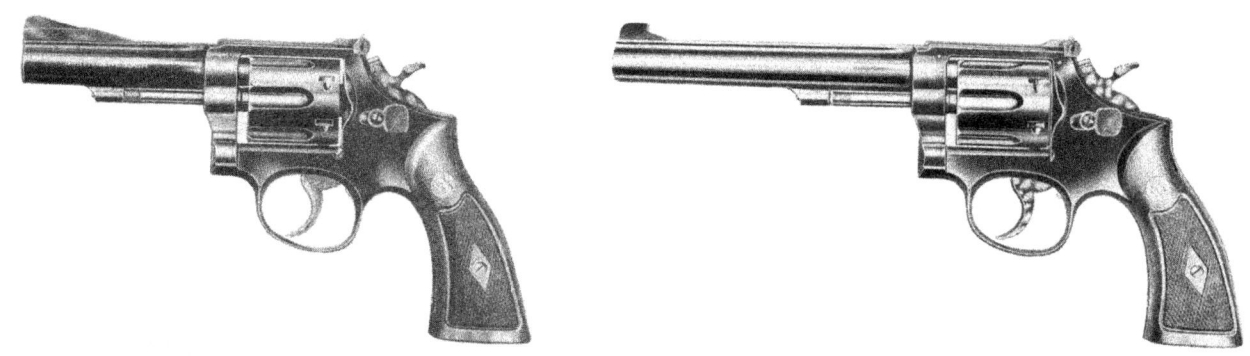

(Left) Smith & Wesson .22 Combat Masterpiece.

(Right) Smith & Wesson K-22 Masterpiece.

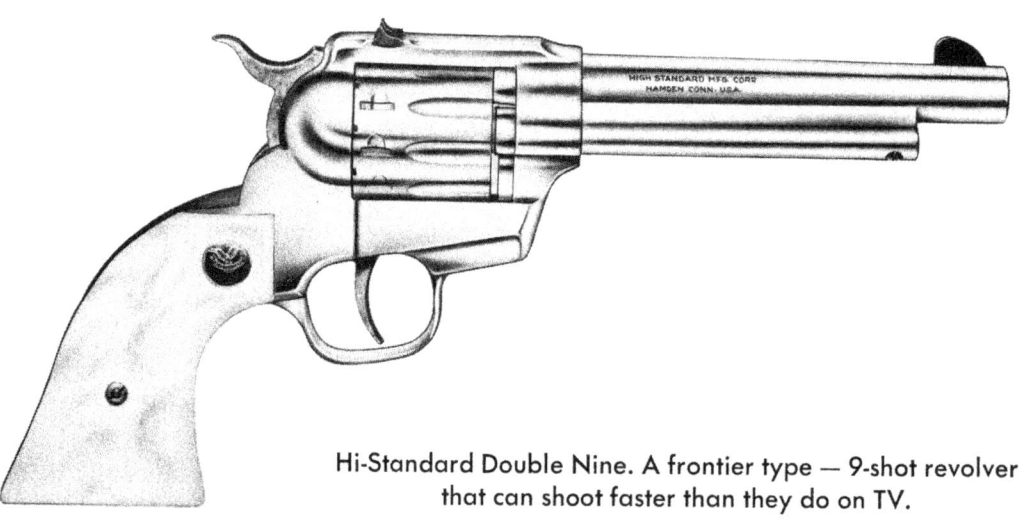

Hi-Standard Double Nine. A frontier type — 9-shot revolver that can shoot faster than they do on TV.

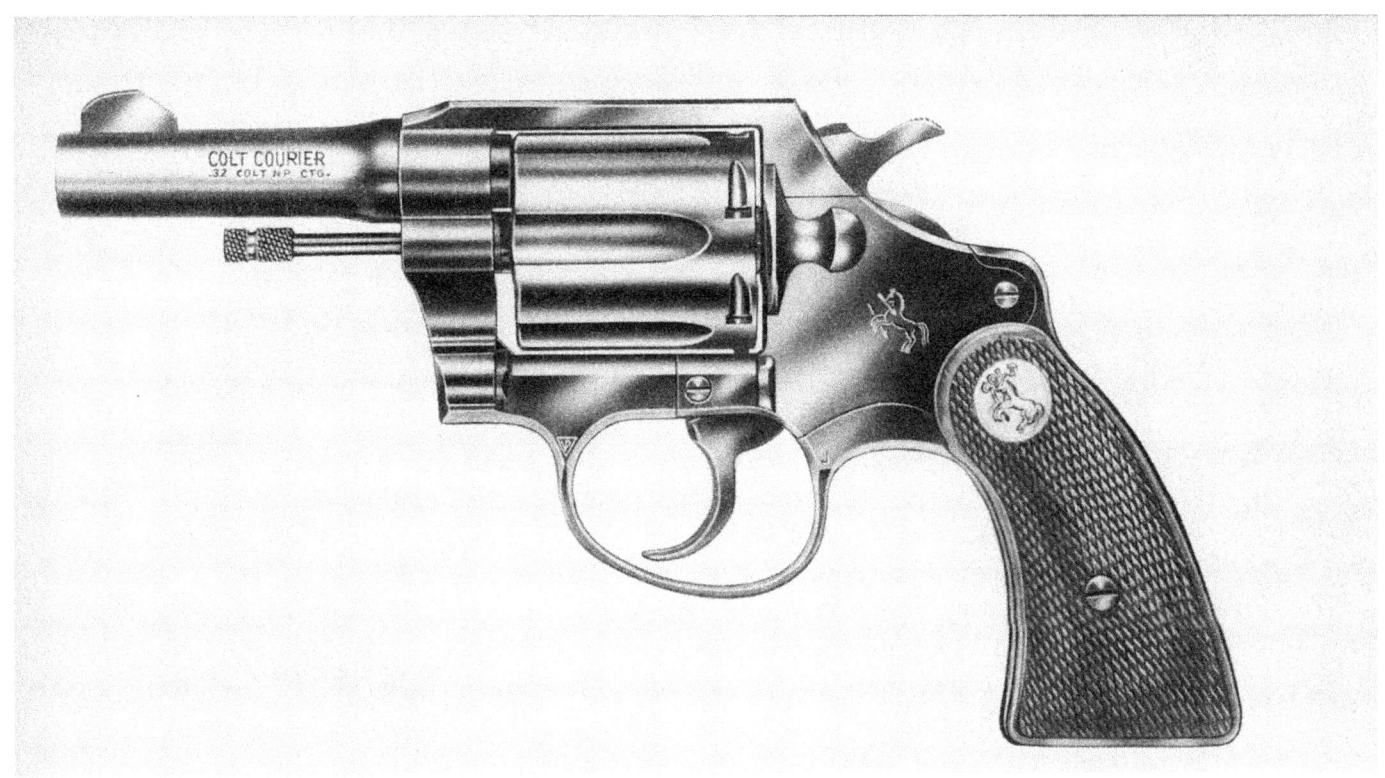

Colt Courier .22

the cutest bit of gunsmithing to come down the pike since Smith & Wesson's Gay Nineties "equalizer," the Ladysmith.

Colt's Frontier Scout is an exceptionally accurate gun, and the Frontier Scout Buntline, because of its long barrel, gets near-rifle performance out of the .22-caliber cartridge. It seems to me unfortunate that Colt makes these guns with the alloy frames rather than the traditional case-hardened steel. A steel frame would make it a much more rugged gun. To me, Colt's Single Action and rugged dependability should be synonymous.

If you want a fun gun with all of the advantages and hang of a single-action, but with none of the drawbacks of the breed, High Standard's new Double-Nine in nickel plate will give you all the romantic feel of the Frontier Six-Shooter, although it is really a nine-shooter. Many plinkers prefer this gun because of its swingout cylinder and the attendant ease of loading and unloading the gun. The fact that it shoots both single- and double-action is reminiscent of the old Colt Lightning double-action revolver, which we always associate with Billy the Kid. An outstanding feature of this gun is its very dependable safety, which functions very much like the safety found on all modern police revolvers. The sleek appearance combined with its low price tag makes it a contender that is hard to beat in the Frontier Fun Gun Sweepstakes.

The K-.22 Combat Masterpiece and the K-.22 give yeoman service as fun guns, as do Colt's .22 Officer's Model Match, .22 Trooper, and .22 Official Police. A few years ago Colt brought out a fine little plinker that it has since discontinued. The Courier .22, with its small butt and three-inch barrel, was a compact little gun for fishing kit or pocket. I felt at the time that Colt should have made that gun with a steel frame instead of the more fragile alloy. Then instead of making the center-fire gun in .32 caliber, if they had made it in .38 special and had the all-steel counterpart in .22 caliber, they would have had a gun that would have been a top seller today.

Gun designer Harry Siefried dreamed up a nine-shot .22-caliber double-action revolver for Hi-Standard that has been hailed as the first "new" gun to be designed in the past fifty years. The "Sentinel" lists among its radical innovations a countersunk ratchet at the rear of the cylinder, a novel and sturdy locking device for the swing-out cylinder crane, a capsule action with the fastest lock time of any modern revolver, and last but not least the best balanced frame and grip since Sam Colt's famed "hawg-leg"! This Hi-Standard Sentinel in nickel plate with a four- or six-inch barrel is in my opinion the best value for your money among the fun guns. Hi-Standard deserves kudos for putting out such a great gun for so little money.

For some reason best known to themselves, some fun gunners prefer to do their plinking with one of the countless semi-automatic .22-caliber pistols available. I hesitate to recommend semi-automatic pistols for this purpose because of the much greater degree of caution required for the safe handling of these guns. Every instance of accidental discharge of a handgun that I myself have been witness to, and fortunately there have not been

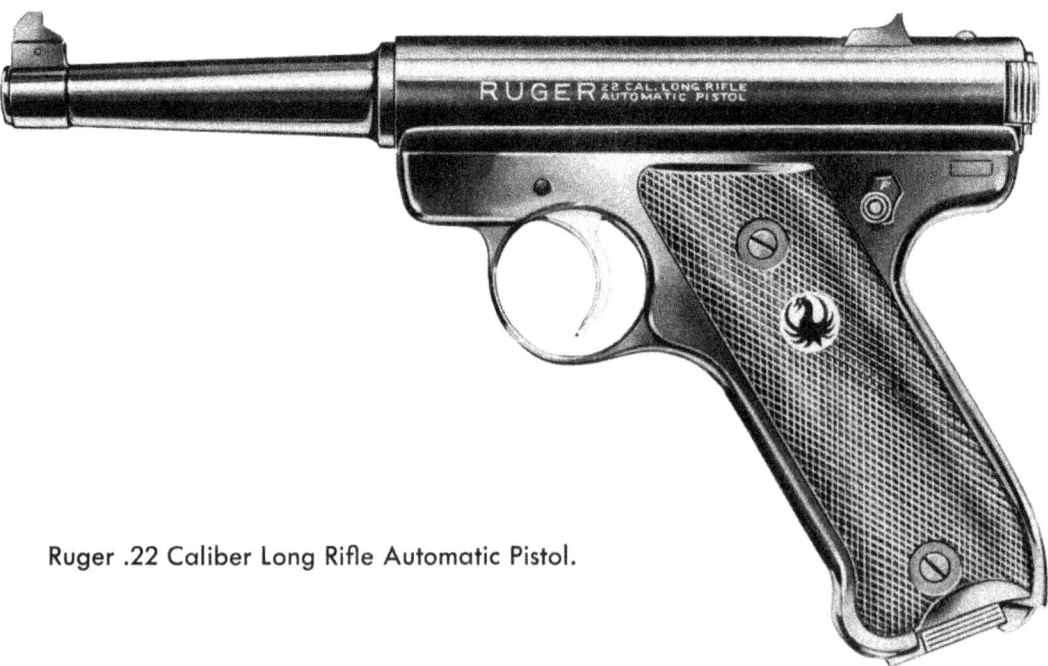

Ruger .22 Caliber Long Rifle Automatic Pistol.

The visible red dot at rear of slide indicates that the weapon is cocked. The red band on the manual safety — at pencil point — indicates that safety is off and the weapon is ready to be fired. *(Right)* The red dot is recessed and no longer visible, indicating the gun is not cocked and cannot be fired.

many, the offending gun was a semi-automatic pistol. It is my personal belief that semi-automatic handguns with exposed hammers are generally safer than the models having concealed hammers. In a gun having an exposed hammer, the shooter can tell at a glance whether the gun is cocked ready for firing or not. One notable exception to this rule is Hi-Standard's economy-priced plinker, the Duramatic, which is available with both long and short barrels that, in effect, practically give you two guns for the price of one. This gun has a protruding bolt showing a red dot when the concealed hammer is in cocked position and a clearly visible safety that shows a red band when the safety is off. Like all Hi-Standard's guns, it gives you more than your money's worth.

The Walther PPK models in .22-caliber are excellent plinking guns, as are the Baretta and Llama pistols. These imports, excellent pocket plinkers though they may be, leave much to be desired in the way of accuracy. The Star Model F is a very well-balanced pistol of surprising accuracy, once you have a good gunsmith go over the pistol and smooth up its rather rough action. From the standpoint of accuracy and safety it is probably the best of the imports. Colt's Woodsman series in .22 automatics are very accurate and are very pleasant pistols to shoot. However, their concealed-hammer

Let everybody have fun; plinking should be a family sport. *(Right)* With a beginner, technique isn't important. Just get the novice to like shooting — formal training can come later.

design does entail an element of risk of accidental discharge. The constant vigilance required for the safe handling of these weapons makes them far less desirable candidates for the more or less casual game of plinking, when there is the so-readily available inherently safe and reliable revolver.

In selecting a fun gun, consideration should be given the other members of the shooter's family who may be using the gun. Plinking can be much more fun when it's a family affair. One of the surest ways to overcome a wife's or mother's objections to firearms is to get them interested in plinking, too. A cautionary word, though — she may prove to be a better handgunner than you are. Children who are taught the safe handling of firearms at an early age are, when properly instructed, far more vigilant in the observance of the rules of safety than are their elders. My son has been around firearms since he was able to walk. By the time he was six years of age, he was so well grounded in the rules of firearm safety that I'd feel safer around him with a loaded .38 than I would around most adults with an empty one.

If the gun is to be used by various members of the family, it should be one that can be safely handled by the weakest as well as the strongest one. The majority of guns today have such stiff, rough, and heavy actions that they would defy a Hercules to shoot them with any real degree of consistent accuracy. Once the internal workings have been de-burred, smoothed, and polished, and the trigger pull lightened to not more than two-and-a-half pounds and a Flaig's Ace Trigger Shoe installed, you will be amazed at your weapon's improved accuracy. With a light, smooth, crisp action, it can be safely handled by a woman or a child old enough to be trusted with a gun.

Many people have asked me how old a child should be before he can be taught to shoot. It depends entirely upon the child in question. If your child is respectful of authority and obedient in your everyday relationships, then he is old enough to learn to shoot under close supervision. An irresponsible child — or adult — should not be trusted with firearms. I know of many eight-year-old boys and girls who derive a great deal of safe pleasure from shooting in the company of an adult. I also know of many thirteen- and fourteen-year-olds who are extremely safe and conscientious hunters and plinkers completely on their own. These youngsters are often far more competent than the majority of adults. Since the NRA Hunter Safety Program became mandatory in New York State and young hunters were required to pass safety tests before they were issued a hunting license, hunting accidents have been more than cut in half and the majority of the accidents reported involved older hunters who had not been required to take the test. Children have a very natural and normal curiosity about firearms. If this interest and curiosity are properly handled, through competent instruction, you may well be averting a tragedy. In the great majority of cases where children have been involved in tragic shooting accidents, they have been forbidden *any* contact with firearms.

CHAPTER 7

Centerfire Hunting Weapons

THE EVALUATION of the .22 handguns made in the fun gun chapter covers all that need be said about the small-bore guns for hunting. In the majority of cases in the field the .22 is not called upon for personal defense although I know of one case where a Hi-Standard .22 automatic pistol in the hands of an Alaskan guide was responsible for a one-shot kill on a Kodiak bear. Many big-game hunters owe their lives to a dependable handgun.

One of the stanchest advocates of a heavy-caliber handgun on a big-game hunt is that dean of American handgunners, Elmer Keith. The redoubtable and controversial Mr. Keith knows whereof he speaks. He has dispatched more than one enraged grizzly who should have had more sense than to tackle Elmer and his heavy handguns. I have heard of African lions being killed with a standard .38-caliber police revolver shooting standard 158-grain ammunition. Still, I wouldn't want to be in the same county with a lion, if I had to count on armament like that. If you invade a big-game country packing anything smaller than a .357 Magnum having at least a six-inch barrel, you'd better be sure that your life insurance is paid up. Maybe you're the sort of hombre who likes to live dangerously.

One of the finest sidearms to take along on a hunt is Smith & Wesson's .357 Magnum with the eight-and-three-eighths-inch barrel. It shoots as straight as a rifle and packs a lot of authority. Colt's .45-caliber Buntline Special with its twelve-inch barrel is another handgun that provides a whale of a lot in the way of long-range accuracy. Ruger's king-size knuckle-duster,

Time invested in introducing your son to handgun hunting can be one of the most rewarding experiences of a lifetime for both of you.

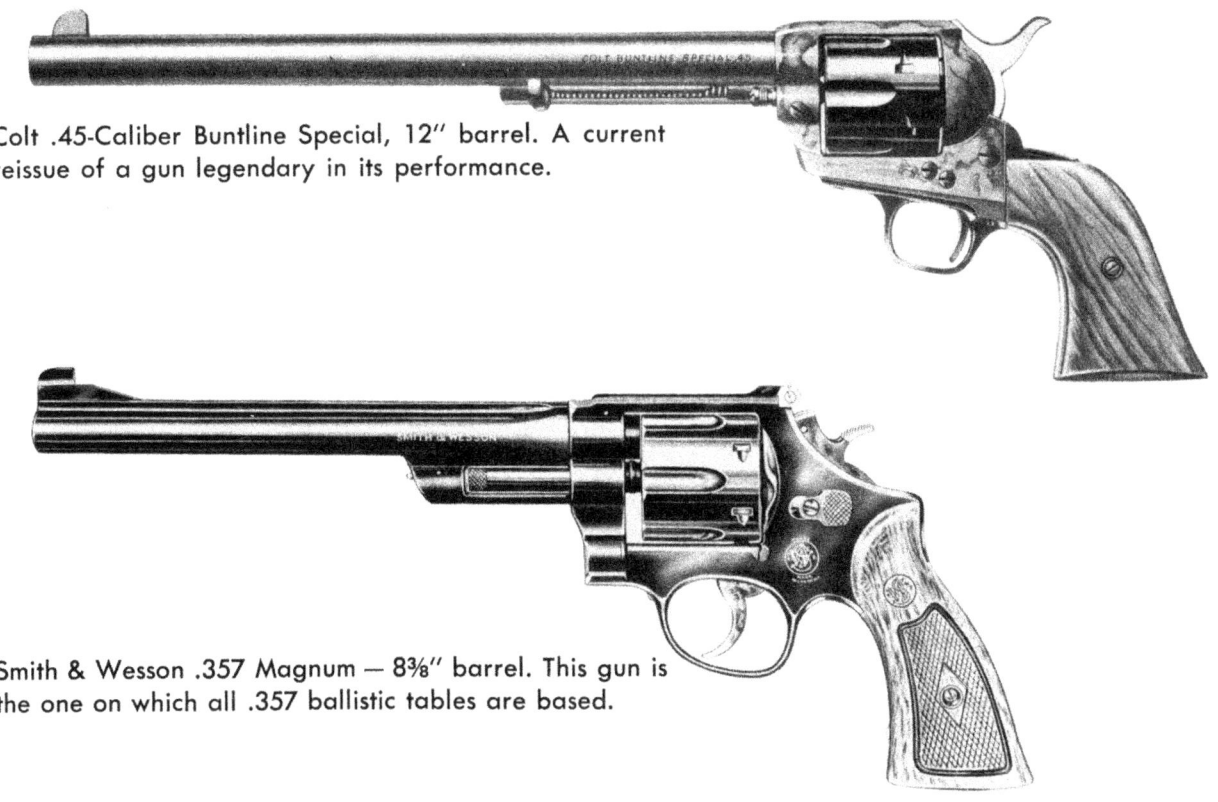

Colt .45-Caliber Buntline Special, 12" barrel. A current reissue of a gun legendary in its performance.

Smith & Wesson .357 Magnum — 8⅜" barrel. This gun is the one on which all .357 ballistic tables are based.

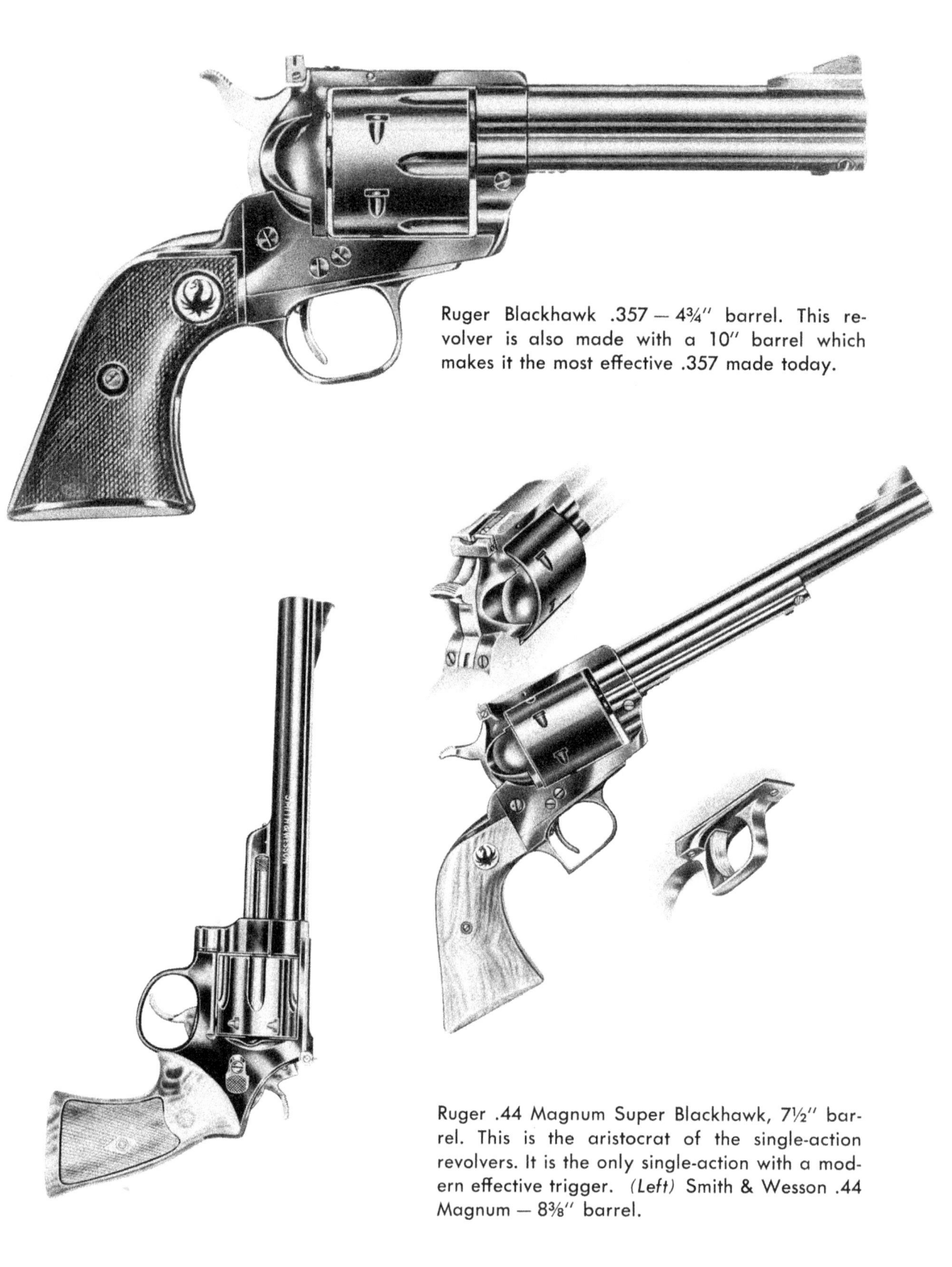

Ruger Blackhawk .357 — 4¾" barrel. This revolver is also made with a 10" barrel which makes it the most effective .357 made today.

Ruger .44 Magnum Super Blackhawk, 7½" barrel. This is the aristocrat of the single-action revolvers. It is the only single-action with a modern effective trigger. *(Left)* Smith & Wesson .44 Magnum — 8⅜" barrel.

the .44 Magnum Super Blackhawk, can be counted on to kill any game animal in the Western Hemisphere. With the exception of elephants, rhinos, and the large African buffalo, the Ruger Blackhawk .44 Magnum with the new ten-inch barrel can handle any animal in the world.

Both Ruger and Smith & Wesson have realized that in the heavy-caliber gun the performance rises in proportion to the length of the barrel. As a result both Ruger and Smith & Wesson have brought out longer barrels. The Smith & Wesson .44 Magnum is now available in an eight-and-three-eighths-inch barrel that makes it a companion piece to the Smith & Wesson .357 Magnum mentioned in the preceding paragraph.

Ruger has recently brought out its Blackhawk revolvers, both .44 and .357, in ten-inch barrels. This makes them absolutely tops in ballistics performance. They are extremely well-made single-action revolvers with fine hang, balance, and accuracy. The Ruger .357 with ten-inch barrel will find much favor with "chuck" hunters.

I give Ruger's single-action .44 Magnum a slight edge over Smith & Wesson's double-action weapon of the same caliber not only because the ten-inch barrel gives it increased bore capacity but also because I feel the time-honored plow-handled grip tends to do a better job of minimizing the extremely heavy recoil than does the grip on the Smith & Wesson gun. Both are very well-made guns. I doubt that many shooters would have the desire to trigger off a .44 Magnum double-action. The ballistics of a .44 Magnum cartridge show it to be an excellent load.

However, both guns made to handle the .44 are, in my opinion, too light, a fact that results in recoil far in excess of what it should be. Another pound of weight distributed around a gun of that size would make it far more effective and pleasant to shoot. When properly holstered, the additional weight would not be noticeable.

We conducted some experiments with a Smith & Wesson .44 Magnum having a four-inch barrel. The recoil was so rough that my friend, who owned the gun, was going to dispose of it. We made some oversize bronze grips for it, which added about twenty ounces to its weight. These grips reduce the recoil of the full Magnum loads to approximately that of a .38-caliber police revolver. My friend is overjoyed with the performance of this weapon, which now shoots as accurately as a target revolver.

In .357 caliber, the figures given on the ballistics tables are those given by the cartridge fired from the revolver having an eight-and-three-eighths-inch barrel. The performance decreases with the shortening of barrel. For this reason, I feel that a six-inch barrel is the minimum length to be considered for use around big game. In this length, I rate Colt's .357 Python as the top performer in its class. The increased weight at the end of the barrel balances the gun in such a way that a very close grouping of shots can be fired with extreme rapidity. This could prove to be a lifesaver in the field.

If you have one of the early Colt New Service revolvers, in .357 caliber, you may consider yourself fortunate indeed. I never could see why Colt halted production of their very fine heavy-frame revolvers. Also, if you should happen to own one of Colt's .357 single-action Frontier revolvers with a seven-and-a-half-inch barrel, you've just about struck gold! My feeling is that as a hunting weapon, Smith & Wesson's Magnums have a slight edge over the standard Colt .357 in current production. The Smith & Wesson 1950 .44 Military Model can be a very effective weapon in the field if you are a handloader, as can the Smith & Wesson .38 heavy-duty .38-44 Outdoorsman. I have seen custom loads that would give these guns top performance in the field. A 200-grain .38-caliber slug moving out at around 1,250 feet per second can be more effective than the standard .357 load. If you are a handloader, and own a heavy-framed .38-, .357-, or .44-caliber handgun, you can tailor your own loads to cope with almost any game you come across. If you have a heavy-frame gun that can stand the high pressures of the hot handloads, you can triple your enjoyment of handgun hunting. I've never seen a handloader who didn't have at least a couple of pet loads he had developed that would solve all the ills of shooting.

The .22 Magnum does not belong with the centerfire guns but I am putting it in because of its power and performance. Both Ruger and Smith & Wesson are bringing out revolvers for this cartridge. Both the K-22 and

Ruger Single Six .22 Magnum caliber, 6½" barrel.

Colt Python .357 — 6" barrel. This revolver has the best balance of all .357's for double-action shooting. Smith & Wesson .38-44 Outdoorsman — 6" barrel.

the Ruger Single Six with a longer barrel are now made for this new cartridge. In a six-and-a-half-inch barrel it has a muzzle velocity of 1,560 feet per second.

Some shooters like some of the heavy-caliber automatic pistols on a hunt. I don't subscribe to this theory myself. The Luger, the 9-mm. Browning, the 9-mm. Smith & Wesson Automatic, and Colt's Super .38 are all reasonably accurate handguns, but because they all shoot a jacketed bullet, they do not produce the degree of shocking power necessary for quick kills on sizable game.

Ineffective automatic pistol loads. None of these produce sufficient shock power.

(Left to right)

Super .38

.380

9mm Luger

.25 caliber

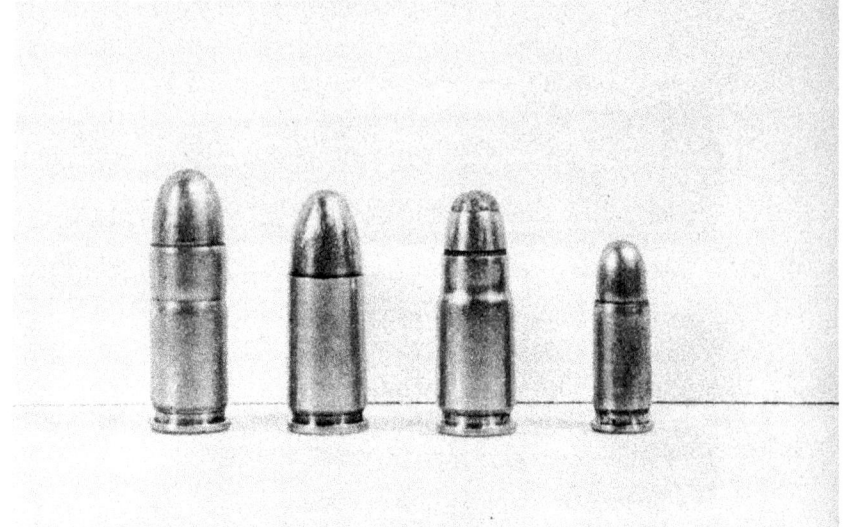

(Left to right) .22 WRM (.22 Magnum); .22 L.R. H.P. Winchester Western Super-X hi-speed hollow-point .22 Long Rifle); Super-X hi-speed .22 short.

CHAPTER 8

Ammunition

READERS OF THIS BOOK may get the impression that I recommend only the most vicious and destructive handguns and ammunitions. I do. You are defending yourself, your property, or the lives or property of others. Trouble may come at any moment. You should be able to handle this trouble effectively and quickly, with the least possible danger to yourself and innocent bystanders.

So I say again and again: *Don't be under-gunned!*

Your handgun should be capable of safely handling loads that will stop a man with a minimum of shots, no matter where you hit him in the body.

SEMI-AUTOMATIC LOADS

In semi-automatic pistols there are only three possible loads to be considered. Of these three, two leave much to be desired. The Colt Super .38 has an extremely high muzzle velocity and relies on this for its killing and shocking power. The 9-mm. Luger cartridge has much the same characteristics.

These two cartridges give you about a 50 per cent chance if the bullet strikes heavy bone. However, since they shoot a jacketed bullet, their destruction of tissue, which produces the nervous shock necessary to put a man out of action, is definitely limited.

. The slower-moving, heavier slug of the Colt .45-caliber ACP is the only semi-automatic bullet that does produce sufficient knockdown and shock.

The Man Stoppers

(Left to right)

.44 Magnum

.45 Keith Hand Load

.45 Colt

.44 Keith Hand Load

.45 A.C.P.

It will take the fight out of your adversary in the majority of cases. Nevertheless, there are cases on record of men absorbing several of these slugs without their attack being stopped.

It is for this reason that the majority of persons carrying a weapon for vital defensive purposes prefer to carry a revolver.

REVOLVER CARTRIDGES

The most desirable calibers for defensive purposes are the .45-caliber Colt revolver cartridge, the .44 Magnum, the .44 Special, and the .44-40. These loads have heavy soft-lead bullets that deliver the utmost in shock and destruction of tissue. Under most circumstances a man hit by one of these bullets almost anywhere in the body will be immediately put out of action.

I even know of one detective who carries a cut-down Colt New Service revolver. He hand-loads his own cartridges and casts his own 300-grain wad-cutter bullets. He does not want ever to have to shoot a felon more than once. To date he hasn't had to fire the gun in the line of duty. One look at his ferocious hand cannon is enough to pacify the most vicious criminal. They just throw up their hands and say. "Don't shoot!" You may think this is carrying things to extremes, but this man will never be in the position of being under-gunned.

The .357 Magnum revolver loses so much of its effectiveness with the shorter barrel length that it cannot be counted on as a sure man-stopper.

The most effective of the medium-caliber loads:

.357

.357 Keith hand load

.38 Keith hand load

.38 Winchester Western 200-grain Super Police

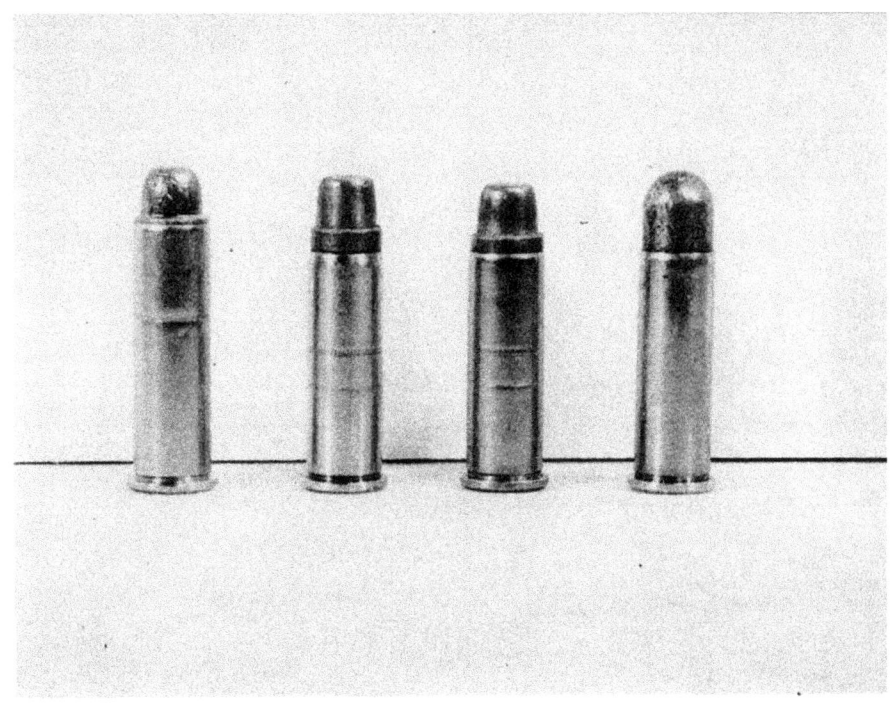

A cop in Rochester shot a man five times with a .357 without knocking him off his feet. Not hitting bone, the bullets just went whistling on through. The cop is now carrying a Single-Action Colt .45.

The .38-.44 is a reasonably effective load, but the .38 "Man-Stopper" using a 200-grain blunt-nosed lead bullet is the cartridge I recommend first and foremost. If ammunition manufacturers would bring out a .357 cartridge using a 200-grain wad-cutter bullet, then we'd have a nearly ideal combat cartridge.

Some peace officers favor the .38 with the hollow-point bullet — the Keith load. This deadly bullet mushrooms and creates a large and exploded wound channel with excessive destruction of tissue. It gets its knock-down power not from bullet weight but from this tearing action and the terrific nervous shock produced. It is so deadly that the majority of police departments frown on its use. There is the possibility of legal repercussions in the event of a wounding or a fatality of an innocent bystander resulting from the use of these lethal projectiles. Prosecuting attorney and attorneys for the plaintiff in damage suits are wont to refer to the hollow-point as a "murderer's bullet."

The regulation .38 Police cartridge is not nearly so effective as it should be for the job it has to do. In one case I know of, a policeman shot a felon three times in vital areas of the body and wound up having to kick him in the head to settle the argument.

I know of one instance where a police officer emptied the six shots in his service revolver at point-blank range into the center of a felon's body.

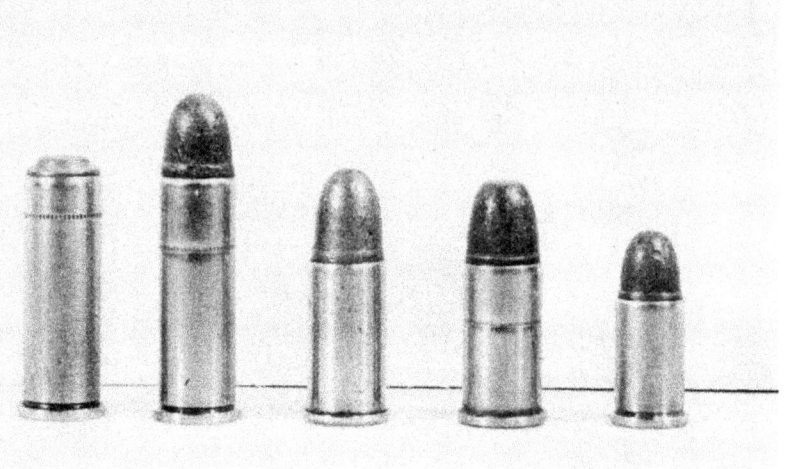

Ineffective .38-caliber combat loads:

(Left to right)

110-grain wad cutter

Standard 158-grain police load

.38 S. & W. New Police

.38 Colt Positive

.32

Hollow-point bullet with two examples of the expansion after having been fired at close range into sand. These bullets are extremely destructive to tissue.

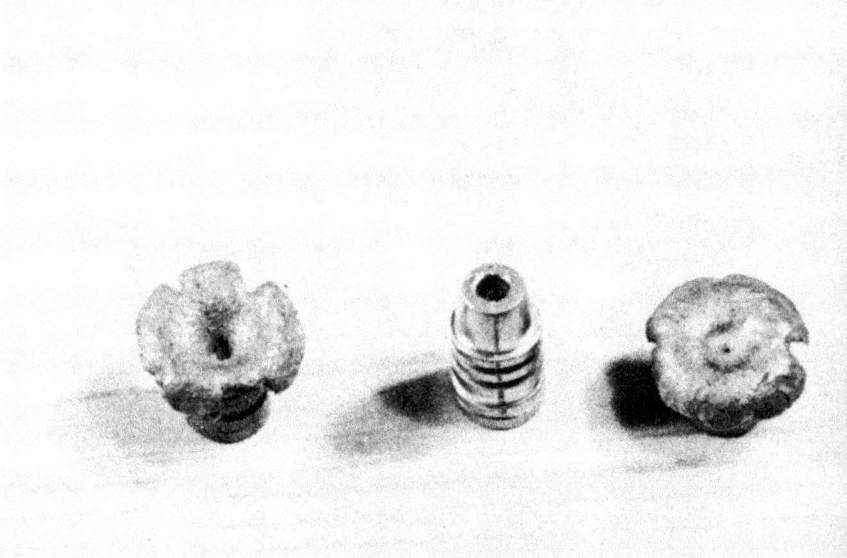

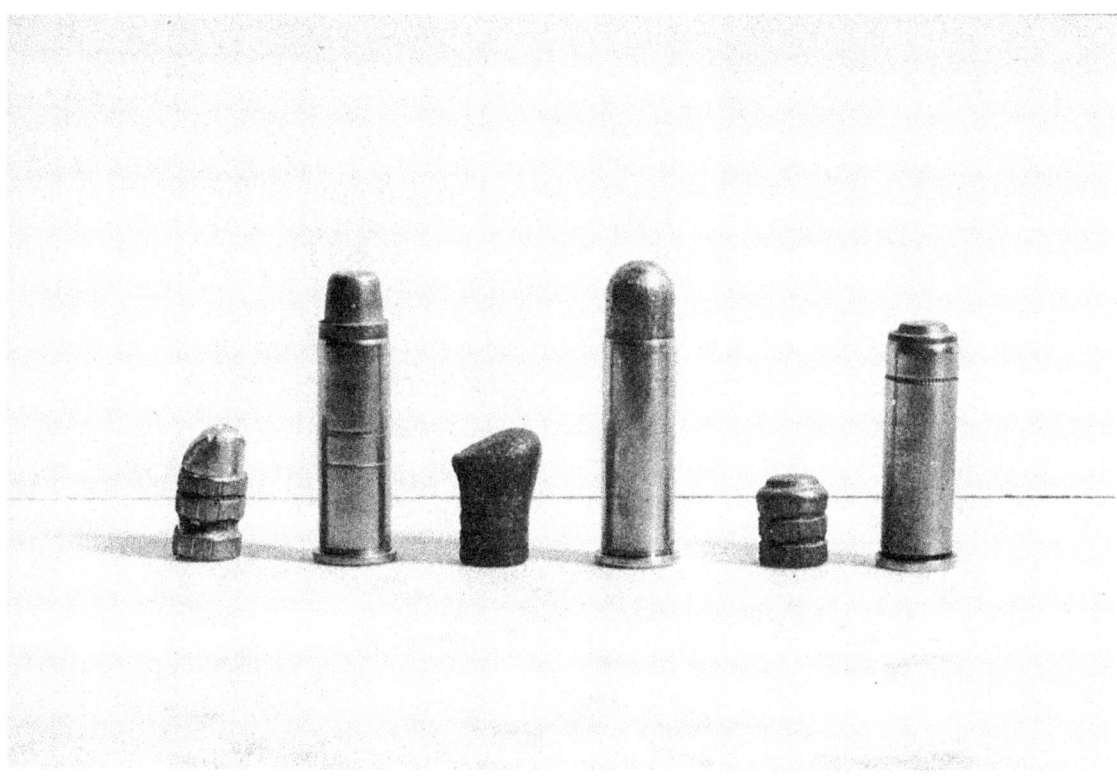

Photo showing the expansion of the bullets after firing into sand at close range. Note that the 110-grain wadcutter is changed in no way. The obvious conclusion is that the 200-grain would be far more effective against a man. *(Left to right)* 1. Keith bullet cast in linotype metal. 2. Winchester Western Super Police 200-grain. 3. 110-grain wadcutter.

The criminal, who weighed one hundred and ten pounds, lived long enough to kill the officer with eight stab wounds before the cop's partner could get to him. One shot from a really heavy-caliber gun would have saved his life.

Psychos and normal people under stress of extreme rage have so much adrenalin pumping through their veins that they are practically immune to normal shock. This condition, which is known to prevail in humans, dogs, monkeys, and bears, can enable a person who is mortally wounded to continue to fight on in seeming contradiction to the laws of physiology.

It is sheer folly to try to defend your life with a gun shooting anything less than the .38 "Man-Stopper." The .38 short, the .32, and the .25-caliber loads can inflict fatal wounds. However, the effect desired is to have a bullet that hits a man almost anywhere in the body put him down and out of the fight fast. To use a bullet of such limited shocking power that it will permit an antagonist to fight back, after having been wounded, is just asking for trouble.

Many detectives carry .32s because of their small size and compact design. Most of them don't realize they are relying on an extremely worth-

Ammunition   67

less gun. There are many cases listed of felons continuing to resist after having been shot half-a-dozen times in the body with a .32. One detective friend of mine, fully aware that his .32 lacked the power to stop anyone with a body shot, found himself in a gun battle with a holdup man and deliberately fired four shots into the man's head. None produced a knockdown effect. The man made his escape. He was wounded, but certainly not fatally: his body was never recovered. He didn't show up in any hospital for emergency treatment. No doctor's report was made of treatment of his wounds. All the evidence seems to indicate that although shot about the head and face at point-blank range, the hoodlum simply did not sustain wounds severe enough to require professional emergency treatment.

THE .22-CALIBER CARTRIDGE

The .22-caliber handgun was designed for sport and target shooting and as a plinking gun while hunting and fishing. Despite its low caliber, the .22 should not be regarded as a toy. More homicides have been committed with weapons of .22 caliber than with all other calibers combined. You should always bear in mind that a .22 high-speed cartridge fires a bullet with slightly greater penetration than a .38 Special.

One of the largest polar bears ever killed was taken with one shot from a .22 rifle. There is even an authenticated case of a .22 handgun killing a Kodiak bear. This animal, which is one of the hardest in the world to kill, was downed with one shot from a .22 Hi-Standard Supermatic.

Both the .22 high-speed and the .22 hollow-point create wound channels that are extremely difficult for a surgeon to repair. The only thing that keeps the .22 from being an ideal defensive weapon is the almost total absence of shock. Because of its extreme accuracy, the .22 is far more deadly than the majority of people realize. When using it for target practice or in the field you should take special care to avoid the possibility of an accident.

The newest addition to the .22 cartridge family is the Winchester .22 W.R.F. Magnum. It is the most powerful rimfire cartridge in current production. This .22 drives a 40-grain jacketed hollow-point bullet from the muzzle of a revolver with a six-and-a-half-inch barrel at a velocity of 1,550 feet per second. Because of its hollow-point construction and its high velocity, it destroys more tissue and tears a wound channel far worse than the standard 158-grain .38 Special.

Velocity and muzzle energy in some cartridges do not mean as much as is generally thought. Unless that energy is used up within the body that is hit, much of the energy is lost. Bullets that completely penetrate the body

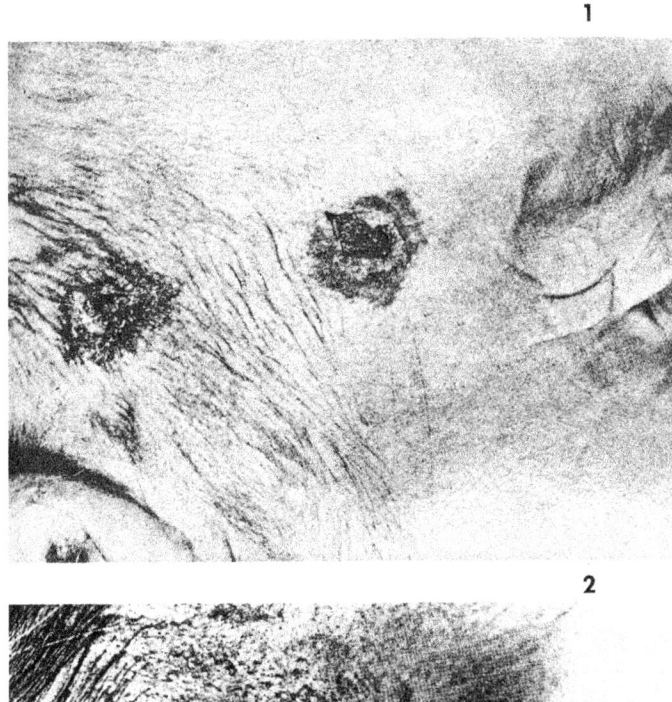

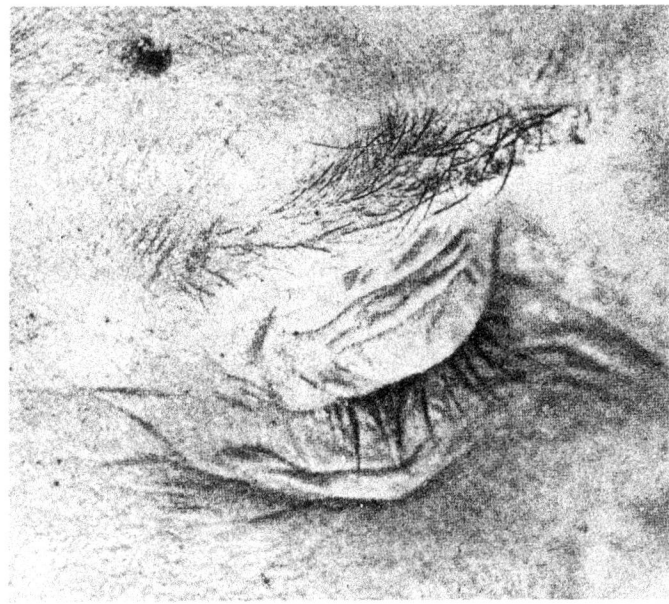

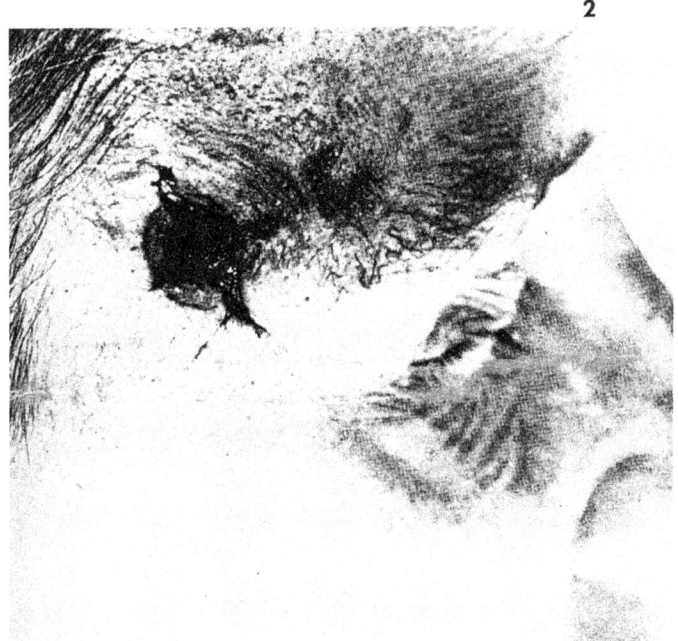

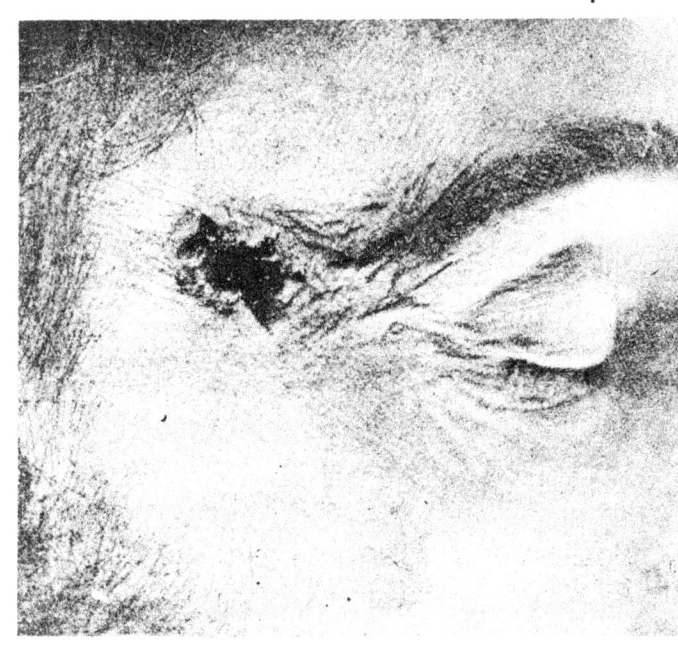

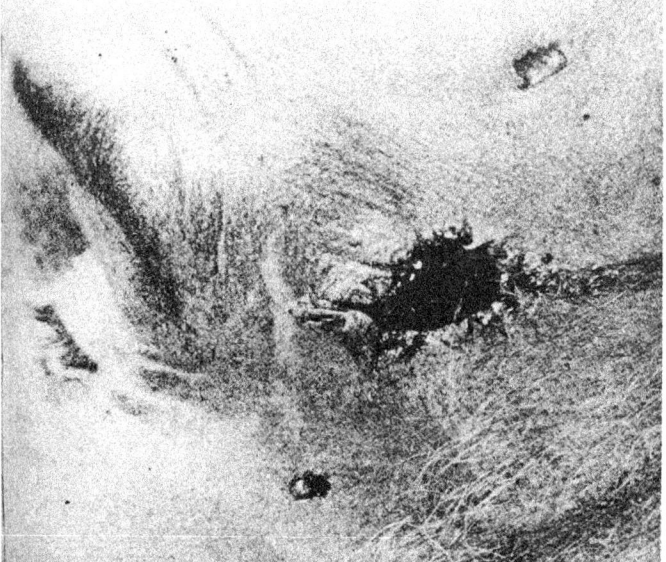

This is a rare collection of pictures of gunshot wounds at contact. It is interesting to note that with the exception of the .44-caliber wound, there is relatively little difference in the size of the entrance wound inflicted by the lower-caliber bullets. The bullet was traveling at the maximum muzzle velocity for each weapon in every case.

(1.) .22 caliber
(2.) .25 caliber
(3.) .32 caliber
(4.) .38 caliber
(5.) .44 caliber

Entrance and exit wounds showing tremendous damage inflicted by a heavy .357 slug.

(Top) Entrance — traveling at maximum velocity.

(Bottom) Exit — the internal damage was extensive before the .357 made its exit.

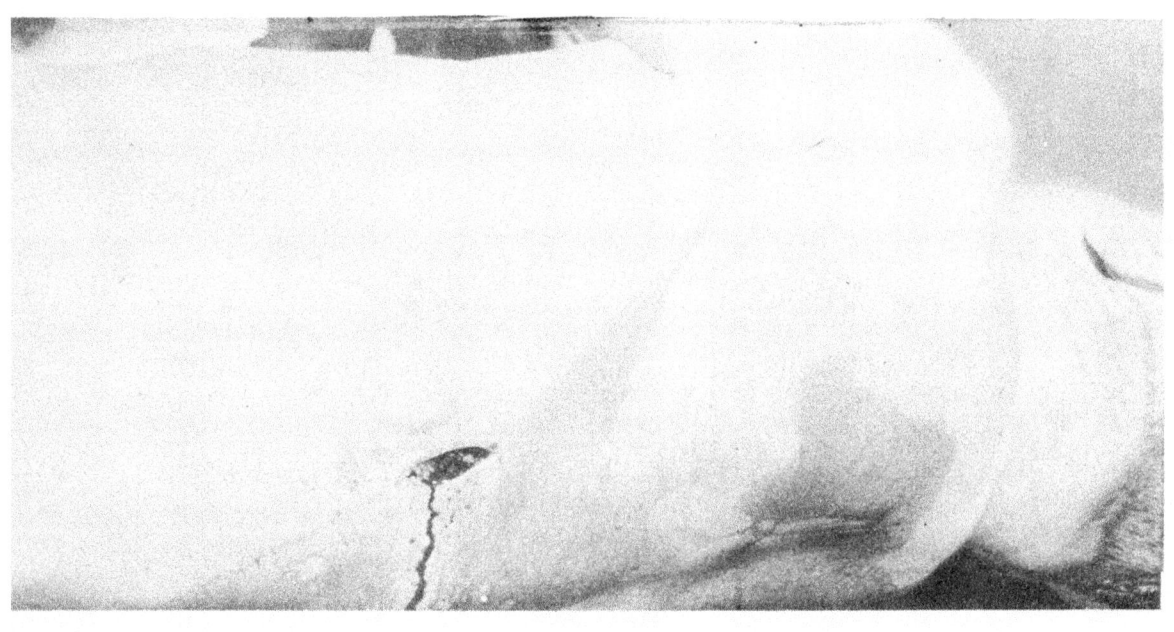

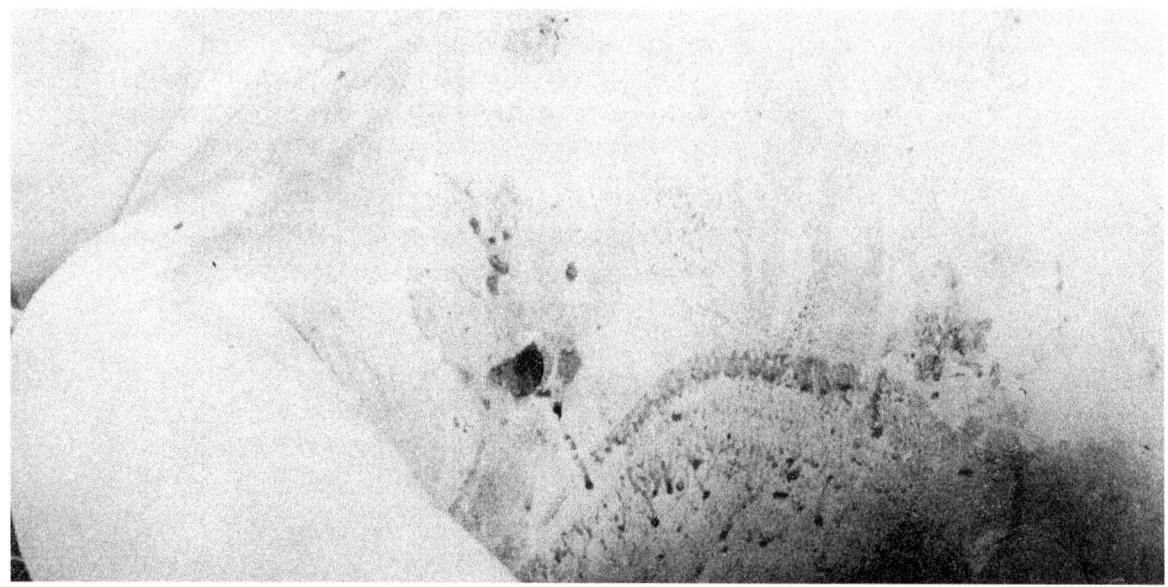

use up only the energy necessary to make their entrance, pass through, and make their exit. For this reason the two important factors in an effective bullet are its weight and its conformation or shape.

A pointed bullet hitting the body at pistol velocity characteristically pierces the body and continues on its flight. This is true of almost all bullets used in semi-automatic pistols. In contrast, the heavy weight and blunt conformation of the Government Model .45 ACP cartridge impart a tumbling action, which is very destructive.

Among all the heavy commercial revolver cartridges, the .44 Special is one of the least effective. And yet when handloaded by a competent loader in the manner recommended by Elmer Keith, it is second only to the .44 Magnum in effectiveness. Many shooters prefer its performance to that of the Big Bertha of the handgun world, the .44 "mangle 'em." This bullet is far more accurate than either the .38 or .357 Magnum.

In factory ammunition the most effective load, of course, is the .44 Magnum. Next in effectiveness is the .45 Long Colt, which has long been one of the most reliable cartridges. It is useful against both cars and culprits.

The adoption of the .38 Special as the prescribed arm for police departments in the majority of cities and states in our nation has amounted to a triumph for organized crime. If a man really wants to put up a fight, a few punctures from the standard .38 Special police bullets won't stop him. Unless he is hit in a vital spot, he'll go on shooting right back. In contrast, one shoulder hit with a .45 revolver will knock a man off his feet and take all the fight out of him.

One great fault with the .38 police weapon is just this. To capture a man who means business, you have to kill him, rather than being able to wound him so effectively as to bring him in.

HAND LOADING

Hand loading will give you a much more effective cartridge, in many calibers, than is possible with commercial cartridges. Correctly chosen bullet, powder, and primer, in the hands of an expert, can produce something very effective indeed.

The book *Six Guns* by Elmer Keith and the *Ammunition Reloading Handbook* by Lyman, the manufacturer of hand-loading equipment, both give detailed information on how to go about loading your own. The formula that Keith recommends for the .44, the .45, the Magnum, and for the heavier frame .38 should be approached with caution. You should start below the powder charge recommended and increase it gradually, watching always for signs of strain on your revolver. Restraint, vigilance and extreme care should be exercised in all hand loading. Carelessness has earned many a right-hand loader a new nickname: "Lefty."

It would be sheer folly to make a souped-up .38 load that would be practical in a Colt's Official Police or New Service, or in Smith & Wesson's .38-44 Outdoorsman and expect to use it in a "K" frame Smith & Wesson, or an air-weight revolver.

The best all-around police bullet for use in the heavy-frame .38 is made in this way. Use regular .38 brass and .357 Magnum primers. Cast the blunt-nosed 200-grain bullet, similar in corformation to the Western Super Police bullet, out of type metal. Load the cartridge with Unique powder, tailoring the charge to suit the length of the barrel of the weapon. The case should be loaded to produce the velocity of between 1,000 and 1,200 feet per second. This load will smash armor plate. It is equally effective against car or criminal.

When you buy a gun, make sure that it is strong enough to handle the .38-caliber 200-grain Man-Stopper. Your dealer may have to order these cartridges for you. They are worth the trouble. In my shop, we often say that anything less than 200 grains is effeminate.

Steel- and copper-jacketed bullets are not so effective as lead bullets of the same weight. Bullets having a flat nose, as in the "wad-cutter," are more destructive than those with pointed noses.

In choosing ammunition, get the most effective load possible for your gun. After all, anyone you have to shoot at isn't likely to be a friend.

CHAPTER 9

Undercover Holsters

THE UNDERCOVER HOLSTER is one worn by a plain-clothes investigator who is working undercover in very close contact with criminals. His identity as a police officer must be hidden. He may not want to reveal the fact that he is carrying a gun. Or he may use the undercover holster as a hide-out rig for a second gun — an extremely salutary practice in many fields of investigatory work.

To be effective, the undercover holster should carry the gun in a position on the body that cannot be detected by the "bump frisk" often employed by hoodlums or their girl friends. Shoulder holsters and belt holsters are too easily detected by a few pseudo-amorous passes. The holster's position should also enable its wearer to reach the gun with reasonable speed.

ANKLE HOLSTERS

The best of all undercover holsters is the ankle holster. Guns the size of the Chief Special or the Detective Special are easily and effectively hidden in this manner. It is an extremely comfortable holster even after as much as eighteen straight hours of wear. You can draw a gun from this rig while seated in a car or in a tavern far faster than from any other type of holster. When seated at a table, the gun can be drawn and held at ready with no one the wiser in case of impending danger. Its ready accessibility counts

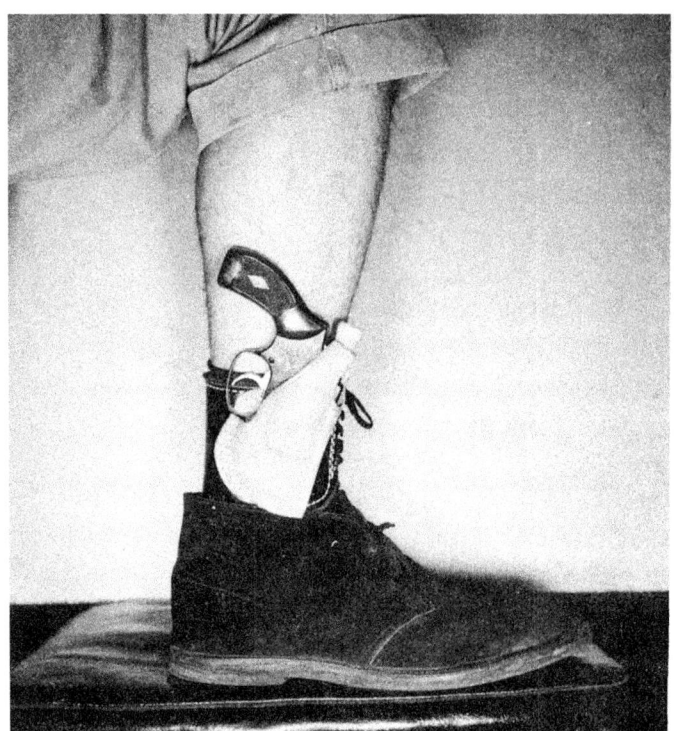 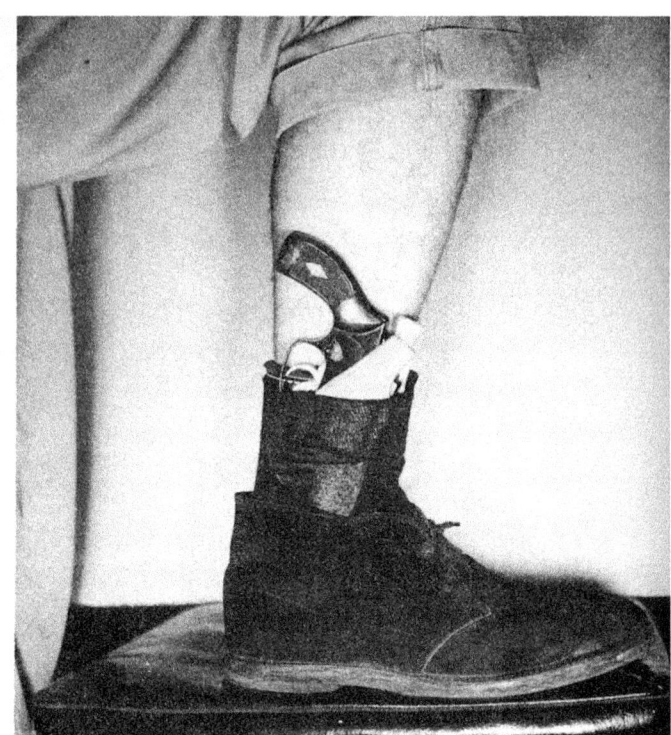

Ankle Holster. Worn with sock pulled up to better camouflage the holster and gun.

heavily when you are wearing an overcoat; and when standing you can draw it nearly as fast as from a belt holster. Many a New York City police officer uses this rig while on duty in uniform. When jumped by a mob of hoodlums and knocked to the ground, he can draw his gun faster than from a belt holster. One of the advantages of this holster is that the officer can wear jeans and a skivvy shirt without fear of being "made."

ARMHOLE HOLSTERS

In climates and urban areas where suits or jackets are worn the armhole holster is an effective undercover holster for very small revolvers, such as *the Smith & Wesson Terrier or small automatics*. This holster is buttoned just below the left armhole. It hangs down inside the left sleeve with the gun in a butt-forward position. The gun can be drawn with reasonable speed, and it will not be detected by a bump frisk. Men working undercover have worn this holster and gone through a regular police frisk without the weapon's being detected.

WRIST HOLSTER

In days of yore, when men wore very wide, heavily starched cuffs, the wrist holster for a small derringer was a pretty item to have around. The way

Left — the crotch holster. This holster buttons onto the suspender buttons sewn inside the waistband of pants.

Right — the armhole holster. This holster buttons into the coat sleeve at the armhole.

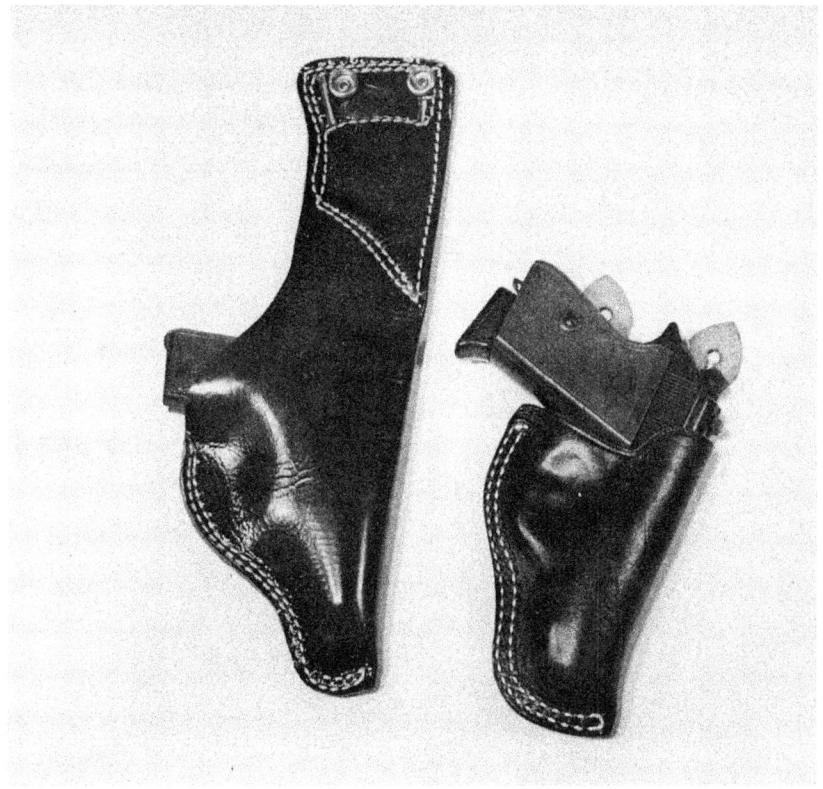

clothing is cut today, however, a wrist holster is a dead giveaway and would be detected in short order by any smart mob.

LEG HOLSTER

This holster is used by undercover men in some less hep areas. It is a terrifically uncomfortable — and usually painful — method of concealing a gun in a place from which it is almost impossible to make a draw in an emergency. Its only virtue is that it does conceal the gun.

CROTCH HOLSTER

The crotch holster is an unusually effective method of concealing a small weapon. It is for extreme cases only, is hard to get to, and is slightly uncomfortable. It is buttoned on to the suspender buttons and is reached by zipping down the trouser fly.

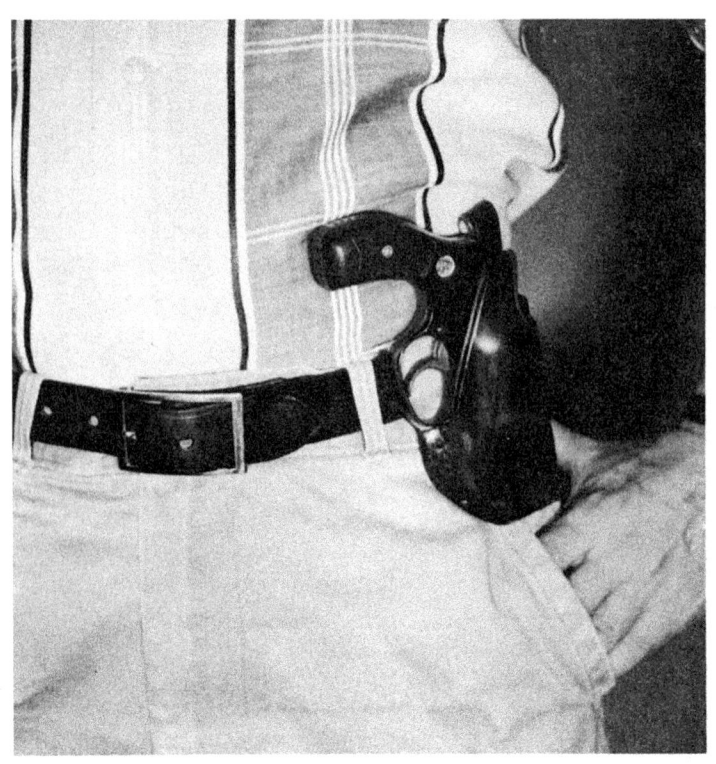
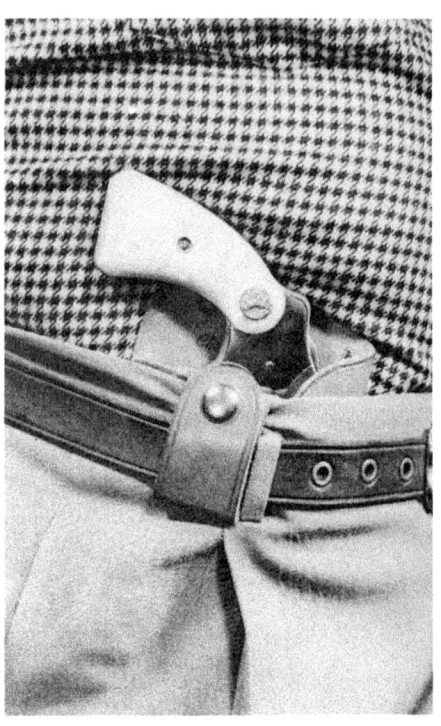

(Right) Super Sleuth Cross-draw holster. *(Left)* Holdout—"inside the pants" holster.

(Below) This Crossfire holster has been designed to be just about as fast as it is possible for a cross-draw holster to be.

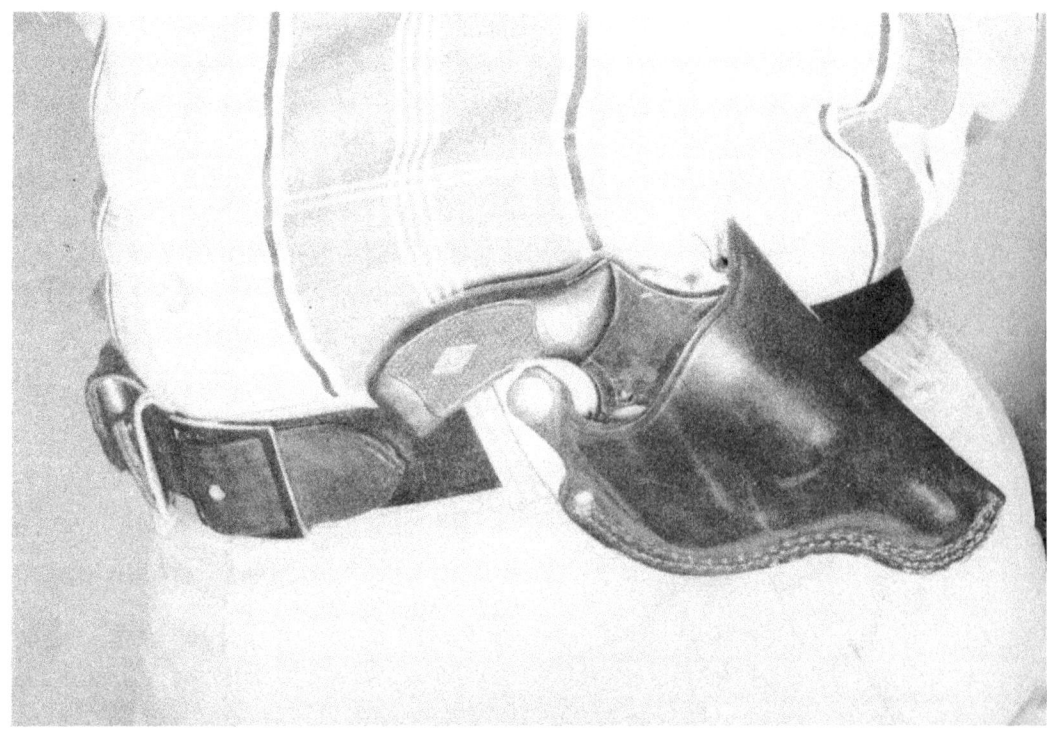

CHAPTER 10

Concealment Holsters

A CONCEALMENT HOLSTER is one that carries a weapon so that an observer cannot see that the wearer is armed. The holster should carry the gun so that it takes advantage of the hollows of the body. The gun should be angled in the direction of the draw. It's been my observation that not one person in a hundred carries his gun effectively in concealment. A good concealment holster should be comfortable and afford maximum concealment for the weapon. *You should be able to draw your weapon from the holster and fire it in less than a second.* If you are a police officer, the elapsed time period should not exceed one-half second.

For almost all conditions a belt holster is much to be preferred over a shoulder rig. An efficient concealment holster should not be bulky, and should be so designed that the gun butt is easily grabbed. The belt loop on the holster should fit snugly the belt the holster is worn on. There should be no movement of the holster, no sliding, slipping, or rocking. A gun invariably should be carried on a belt at least one inch wide and made of very thick leather. No gun larger than the Colt Detective Special or the Colt Police Positive Special should ever be carried on a one-inch belt. A thick one-and-a-quarter-inch belt is ideal for most medium-gun wear. A one-and-a-half-inch to one-and-three-quarters-inch belt should be worn when holstering big revolvers. The belt should be worn tight enough so that after you pass your thumb between your body and the gun butt the butt will snap back and press against the body.

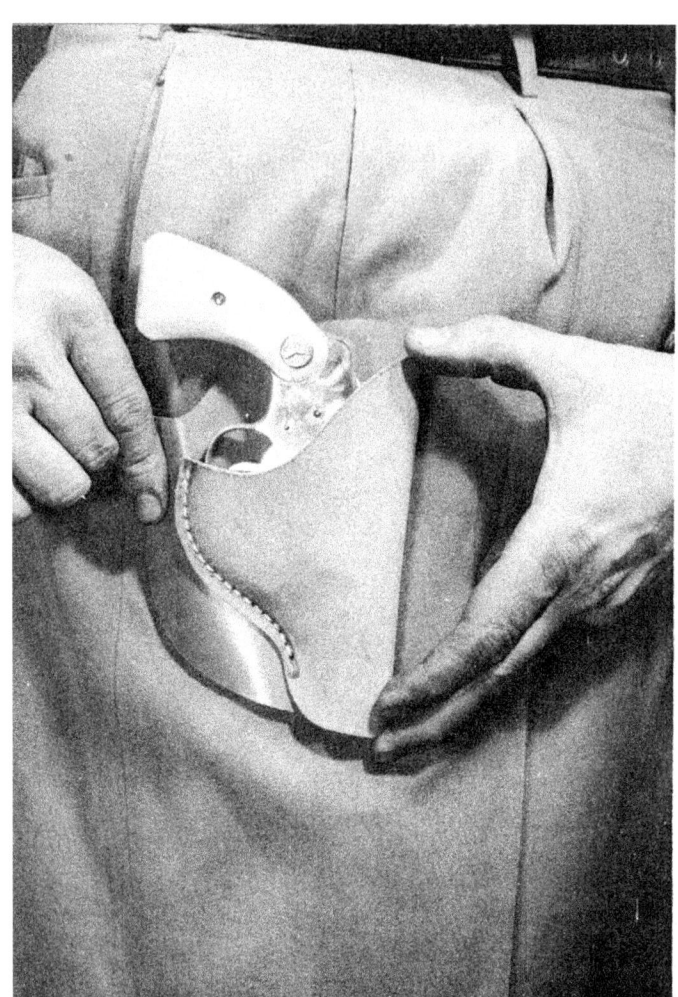 

(Left) 8-Ball side-pocket holster. *(Right)* The Dynamite shoulder holster for snub-nosed revolvers.

I have never seen a completely satisfactory cross-draw concealment holster, and I have designed many a cross-draw rig. When held at the proper angle for an across-the-body draw, the gun does not conform to the body and protrudes enough to make any concealment well-nigh impossible. If the gun is holstered so that it is concealed well, it is awkward to draw. Since cross draw is far slower than a draw should be, I always try to convert novice shooters to the more sensible and practical hip draw.

One of the most practical of all concealment holsters is the "inside-the-pants" holster for revolvers. For all semi-automatic pistols, it is the only one I wholeheartedly recommend. The inside-the-pants holster should have a flap of leather extending upward from the well of the holster, between the gun and the wearer's body. Any other version of this holster is dangerous. This flap not only protects the gun from perspiration, but also is more comfortable for the wearer. However, the most important factor is one of safety:

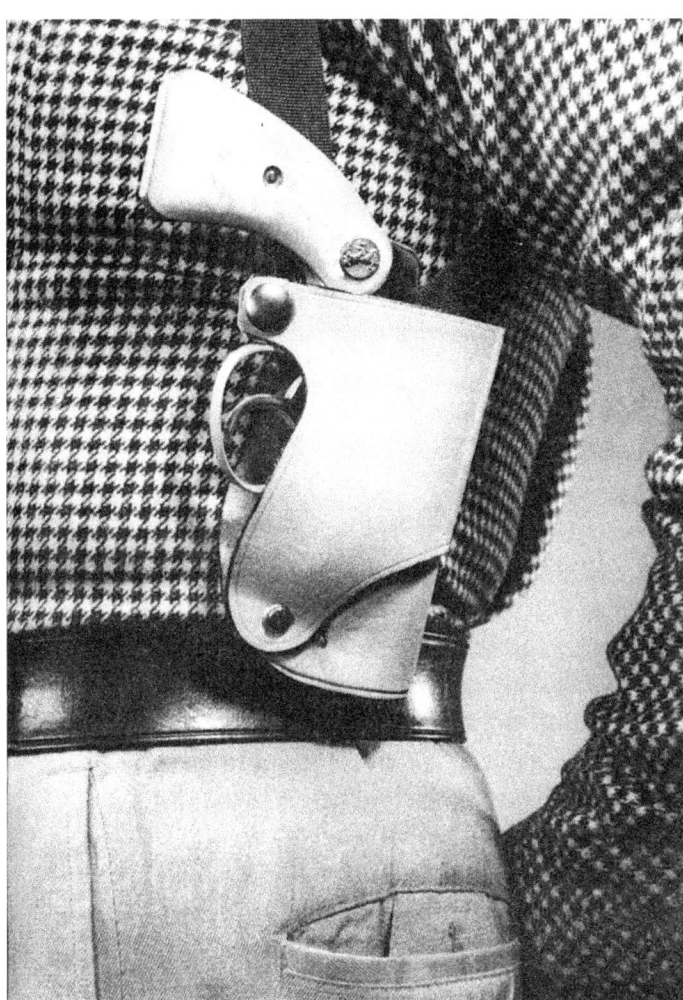 

(Left) Blue Streak shoulder holster. *(Right)* Federal Speed Scabbard shown with a Smith & Wesson Military & Police 4" barrel.

it prevents the revolver hammer from becoming fouled in the shirt during the draw.

Some inside-the-pants holsters have metal clips that are intended to hold the holster to the pants or belt. Too often in a fast draw the holster comes out with the gun. This can have permanently fatal results. The most practical inside-the-pants holster has a tab that snaps securely around the belt. It is easily removed, but secures the holster safely in place. Most people make the mistake of wearing this holster toward the front of their body where it tends to be uncomfortable. It should be worn directly behind either the right or left hipbone. Even extremely large target automatics can be carried with great comfort and concealment in this fashion. For all revolvers, with the exception of the heavy-frame Magnum or guns having adjustable target sights, an inside-the-pants holster is one of the most practical and useful of all holsters. No peace officer should be without one in his locker.

For the past century there have been countless pocket holsters designed. All of these were designed to fit in the hip pocket — a fact that made them useless as a concealment holster. (In case you haven't looked lately, that's a definitely protruding part of the body.) The logical pocket in which to carry a small gun is the side pants pocket. It affords both comfort and concealment. When you're standing in a casual manner, with your hand in your pocket, it affords one of the fastest and sneakiest draws possible. Many a bandit intent upon sticking up a jewelry or liquor store has died with an incredulous look on his face after running up against a side-pocket job.

When people think of concealment holsters, going back to the days of Ben Thompson, they think of shoulder holsters. Except for use with small, compact revolvers, the shoulder holster went out with high-button shoes. For all practical purposes, belt holsters are faster, more comfortable, and more concealing than the majority of shoulder rigs on the market. For a small gun a shoulder holster does, however, offer certain advantages on two occasions: first, in the winter when you are wearing an overcoat; and second, as in the case of diplomats, who must dress formally and carry a gun with the coat buttoned.

The Berns-Martin "Lightning" upside-down shoulder rig for snub-nosed revolvers is a well-designed fast holster, although it sacrifices some concealment and comfort because of its harness.

I have designed two shoulder holsters. The Dynamite, a horizontal directional draw holster, is for small-frame snub-nosed revolvers having small butts. This holster is as comfortable as a shoulder holster can be. It affords an unusually high degree of concealment even when worn with snugly fitted formal attire. This is undoubtedly the fastest shoulder holster made. I designed it originally for policewomen. However, diplomats, heads of state, and our best-dressed detectives went for it to a much greater degree than did their sisters-in-arms.

My other shoulder holster is the Blue Streak. This holster was designed for the Detective Special and the Police Positive Special. It affords a great deal of concealment and is as comfortable as a shoulder rig can be. Its speed, though less than the Dynamite, is on a par with the "Lightning" holster. The Blue Streak holster is favored by detectives working in areas where there is a heavy incidence of mugging. Its two-piece design is in itself a deadly "secret weapon" against this cowardly type of criminal attack. When a hoodlum applies his mugger's choke hold, all the plain-clothesman has to do is grab the gun butt, pivot the gun in a horizontal position and pull the trigger. The mugger's heart is in direct line with the bullet.

There are many shoulder holsters on the market. Unfortunately, it

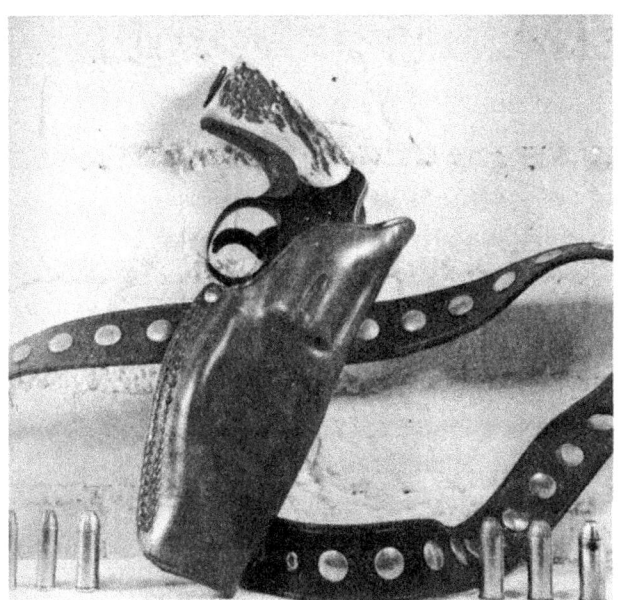 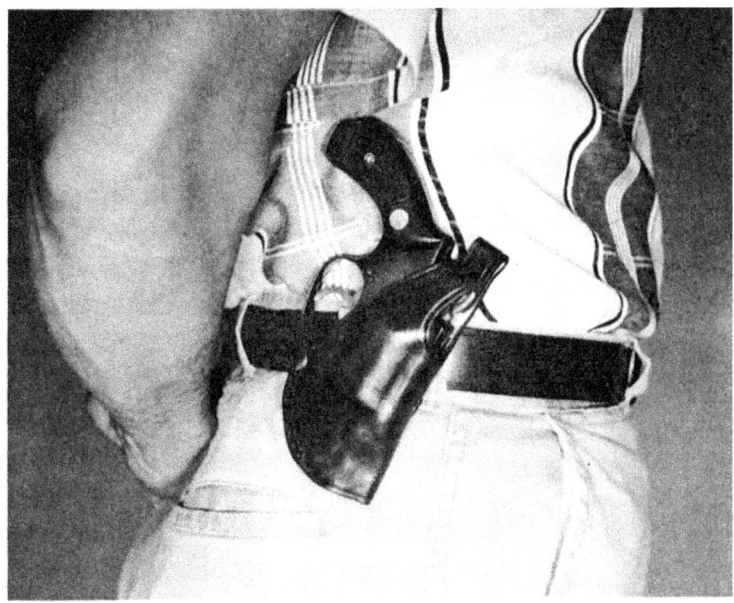

(Left) Formed scabbard for the Colt New Service .45. *(Right)* Super Sleuth, a safe, fast, comfortable and concealing right-hip draw holster.

seems to be a case of each manufacturer copying the other's mistakes. They are much too bulky and do not hang in a way that affords concealment. So much leather is used in them that it is impossible to get a grip on the gun when you make your draw. These holsters are made for guns of all sizes, shapes and descriptions — consequently, they hold none of them properly. These heavy leather harnesses are hot to wear and become "gamey" in short order. They creak like an old saddle, an audible tip-off that the wearer is armed. They have chafed many an armpit painfully. My idea of poetic justice would be to sentence the manufacturer to wear one of these things for a few weeks. One major drawback to all shoulder holsters is that in a rough-and-tumble fight a man can grab your shoulder harness from behind and fling you all over the precinct and you can't do a thing about it.

The right-draw, high-riding holster is the workhorse of the police world; worn just slightly behind the right hipbone, this holster, when properly designed, carries the gun in perfect balance and presents the grip for a fast draw. It does not interfere with the normal use of trouser pockets. Because of its perfect balance ,even an extremely heavy gun can be carried without your becoming conscious of the weight. I know of many instances of detectives carrying .44 Magnums in my Undercover Scabbards, perfectly concealed under a sports shirt. With this type of holster it is extremely important for it to be properly designed for the gun and well made to fit the gun. This is especially true of scabbards.

The scabbard that is issued to the FBI and copied with varying measures of success by most holster manufacturers is a perfect example of what this type of holster should not be. The qualities that a holster of this type needs are concealment, comfort, safety, and fast draw. These commercial rigs have none of them. It is designed so that the overly large belt loop drops the cylinder on the protruding hipbone, thus placing the widest part of the gun on the widest part of the hip. The holster is made to hang almost straight up and down, throwing the butt outward where it is easily noticed. This also positions the gun so that it inflicts maximum wear on the clothing of the agents. The belt loop is extremely wide and there is motion of the gun and holster. This makes the wearer aware of the weight of the gun. In a fast draw the holster slips and slides on the belt, which slows down the speed of draw. As to safety, these holsters are made with a thick divider running down the spine of the holster. This reduces the bearing surface of the holster on the frame of the revolver, making a snug friction fit impossible.

With a properly fitted scabbard you should be able to turn the holster upside down and shake it without the gun falling out. At the insistence of some FBI agents, I designed a scabbard to fulfill the requirements of their job. It is much higher, placing the cylinder directly at the belt level, which puts the widest part of the gun in the narrowest part of the body. I canted the butt of the gun to conform with the line of the body and to afford a fast grip and line the gun up for fast draw. The barrel of the gun, fitting snugly against the hip, keeps the butt snug against the body. I put a coat protector guard over the hammer, which, combined with the gun butt's being hugged into the body, minimized wear on the lining of jackets. The holster is formed so snugly around the gun that bulk is reduced to the minimum and a tight friction fit results. The belt loop fits tightly on the belt, so that no motion of holster on belt or gun in holster can cause discomfort. A much faster draw results because of the absence of slippage. This is the most practical concealment rig for plain-clothes use. Holsters of this type can be made for almost any double-action gun with barrel not exceeding six inches.

Spring holsters are not too satisfactory because the guns must be pulled through the bulky spring with a jolting rocking motion and do not come out cleanly into the line of draw.

The Berns-Martin Speed Holster is frequently bought as a concealment holster. However, the position in which the gun is held, combined with the bulk of the holster, does not make it a good rig for concealment. It is reasonably fast, though not so fast as a scabbard. It is one of the few holsters made to fit snugly on the belt, which makes it both comfortable and stable. One major drawback is the loud popping sound when the gun is drawn. I know of one case where a group of federal agents was sneaking up to surround a covey of felons; as one slipped his gun out of his Speed Holster, the pop of the spring snapping back together was so loud in the stillness of the night that it flushed the feds' game, who then fled into the night. It took several months of hard work to round them up again.

There are many possible versions of retaining devices. Retaining straps that go over the trigger guard are not so desirable as ones that go over the hammer. A strap over the trigger guard becomes too easily fouled between the hand and the trigger guard in an emergency-inspired fast draw. Also, it is possible for a gun to be discharged in the holster when the strap goes over the trigger guard. This cannot happen with one passing snugly over the hammer. Long retaining straps are not so efficient as very short ones. The long strap becomes too easily fouled in the notch behind the hammer. I have found that the best retaining device is a very short one that passes over and covers the spur of the hammer. It is possible to have a retaining strap on your holster designed in such a fashion that the strap can be released and the gun drawn with only a shade less speed than a free scabbard.

So before you buy a holster, think out the requirements of your particular job and decide what the holster must do for you.

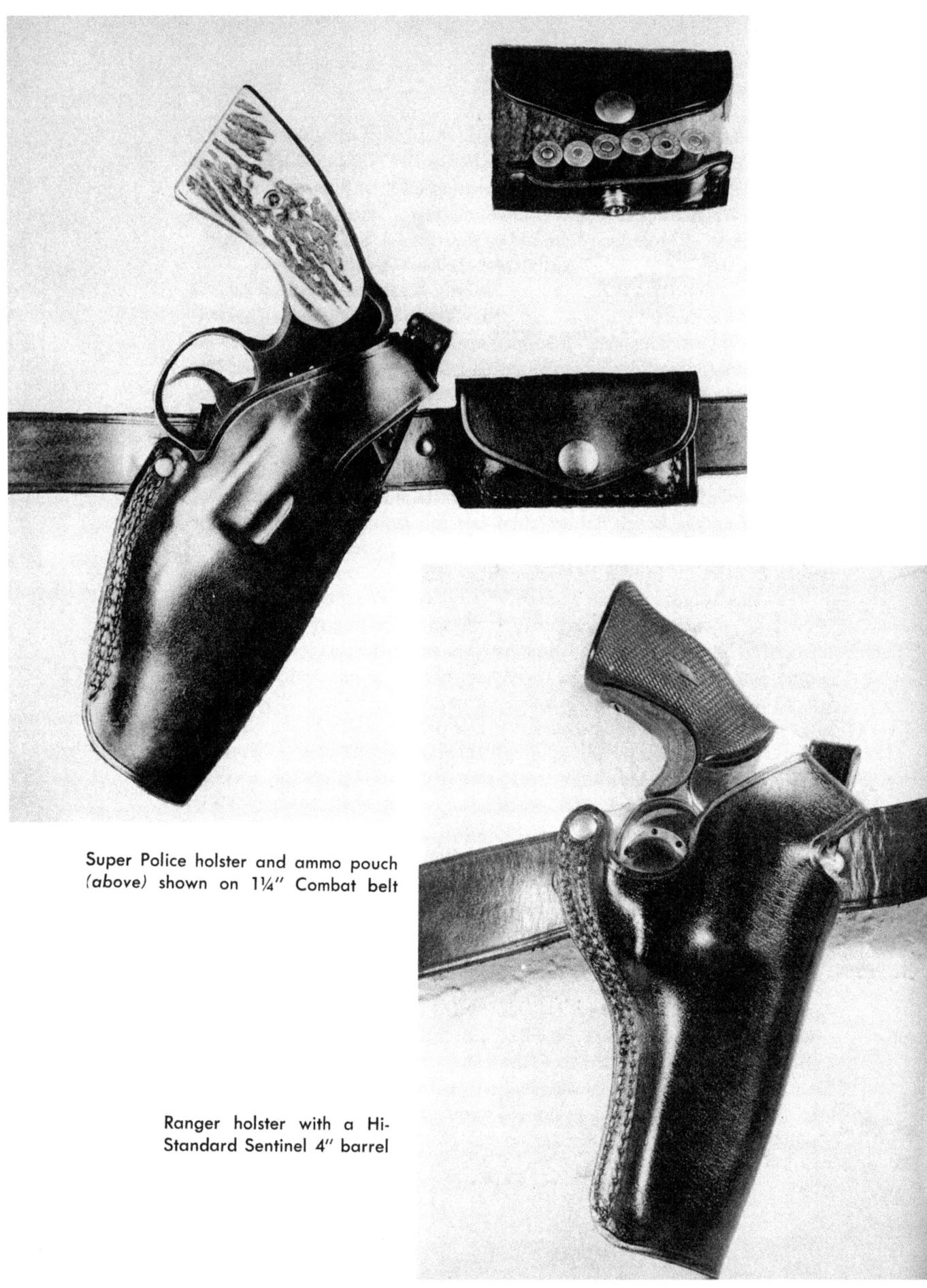

Super Police holster and ammo pouch (above) shown on 1¼" Combat belt

Ranger holster with a Hi-Standard Sentinel 4" barrel

CHAPTER 11

Service Holsters

WITH A FEW happy exceptions, the military and the police of this nation, like those of all other nations, are hampered rather than helped by the holsters issued to them for their use. The trouble is that as a rule designers and manufacturers of holsters have never had to carry a gun for any extended period of time. They know little and care less about the problems of the man who has to live with a gun. Almost without exception, government purchasing agents — whether city, county, state, or federal — buy weapons and holsters strictly on a price basis. They fail to take into account the safety and comfort of the men who have to wear them.

It is, simply, a waste of the taxpayers' money. Wherever possible, an intelligent man will buy his own equipment and throw the issue misfit in his locker. That man is lucky. Some departments and the military insist that their men endanger their lives by using bargain-basement issue equipment. I know of one state and two federal law-enforcement agencies where the holsters are so ill suited to the men's needs that *not one of them is ever used*. The issue holster is either thrown away or consigned to a locker.

A good service holster is one that can be carried comfortably throughout an officer's tour of duty. He should be able to draw the weapon with one hand in any circumstance — whether he is riding in his car, walking, running, climbing, or even, if necessary, hanging upside down. A good service holster should be safe. The weapon should be retained in such a fashion that it can't be snatched away in a fight. It should be so ruggedly constructed that the holster can't be ripped open down the seam.

The Police Department of the City of New York (unfortunately, in this instance it is copied by thousands of smaller communities) has a regulation holster that is about the worst I have ever seen. Usually made of shoddy split leather and lined with canvas that holds sufficient moisture to insure the gun's rusting, this holster seems to have been constructed to be replaced every year. Consisting of innumerable pieces of leather stitched together with cheap cotton thread, it has a breaking point below that of a grocery string. When this holster is brand-new, a police officer has to struggle with two hands to draw the gun. Anybody else with the desire to can get it simply by grabbing the butt and ripping it out of the holster. After it's been out in a couple of rainstorms, the holster comes sufficiently unstitched so that anybody can easily lift the gun out of the holster. I know of one officer on post who heard somebody come up behind him — and turned around to stare down the muzzle of his own gun in the hands of a grinning psycho. Police officers who have Smith & Wesson revolvers frequently find when they have drawn their gun from this holster that the cylinder latch has opened and they have to pick their ammo up off the street before they can do any shooting at all. Police officers have been killed or crippled for life because of the malfunctioning of this holster.

Another bad service holster is a swivel type with a metal trigger lock. This holster is duck soup for any sneak who wants to come up from behind and take the gun. The trigger lock is released by placing the index finger inside the trigger for the release, which has sometimes resulted in officers shooting themselves in the leg or foot. This is especially liable to happen in cold weather when numbed hands can't distinguish between the release and the trigger. I know of one instance involving such a holster when the gun in it went off as its wearer jumped to the ground from a four-foot platform; his leg and foot were so mangled by the shot that he had to retire from the force.

There is a service holster currently being made that springs open like a jack-in-a-box when a button release is pressed. This proves disastrous when hoodlums or small boys learn the secret of its operation. From then on the officer spends a good share of his time picking the gun up off the street. Also, under the stress of combat a gun too often is fumbled, many times with serious results. Gimmick holsters are a sorry answer to the need of the uniformed officer.

A rigid scabbard angled for a fast draw, with a safe but fast retaining strap, is the best holster for service use. It is far faster than any holster relying on the mechanical action of springs, button releases, etc., to release the gun before it can be drawn. A properly designed service holster should be just as fast as the fastest man who will ever use it. The conditions under

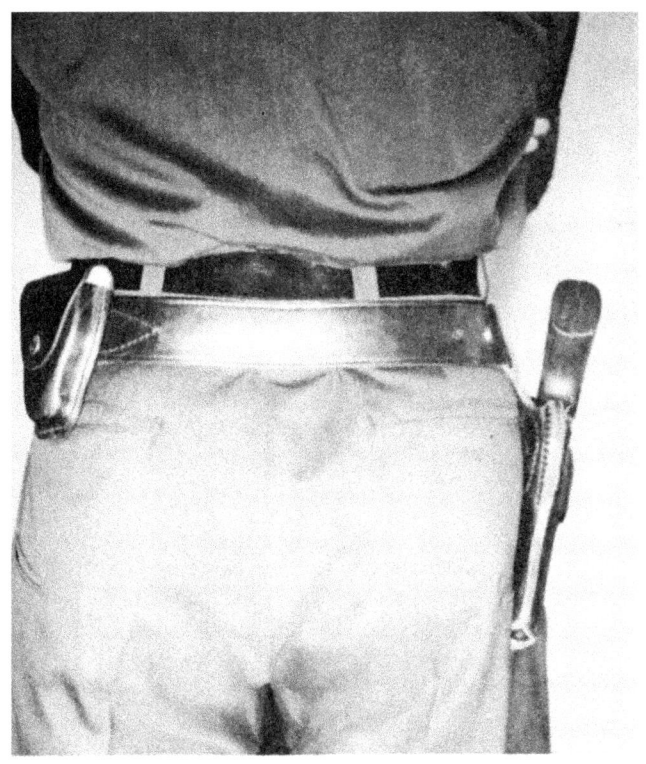 

The Highway Patrol holster and belt.

This holster features a steel-reinforced shank and is tilted just high enough so the wearer can sit at desk or in car.

which we live and work today are such that more and more police officers and military personnel spend a major part of their time riding in cars or sitting at desks. For this reason, a high-riding, forward-tilted holster is more satisfactory than the conventional low-hanging police holsters seen around today.

Except in instances where police officers are patrolling alone in cars, the right-side hip-draw holster is to be preferred. For the man who is on patrol alone and must of necessity transport prisoners sitting beside him in the car, a high-riding cross-draw holster, worn on the left side of the body, has some advantages. This would be unnecessary if police officers would always handcuff their prisoners behind the back.

The United States Border Patrol is one of the few police organizations that issues its men a good holster, well designed to aid, not hinder, them in the performance of their duties.

I have yet to see a service holster issued to any branch of the armed forces that was not fifty years behind the times. The GI holster for the Colt A.C.P. is clumsy, uncomfortable, slow, and extremely hazardous to wear under conditions of modern warfare. This holster is not much different from the ones used during the Civil War. In this motorized, jet, and atomic age

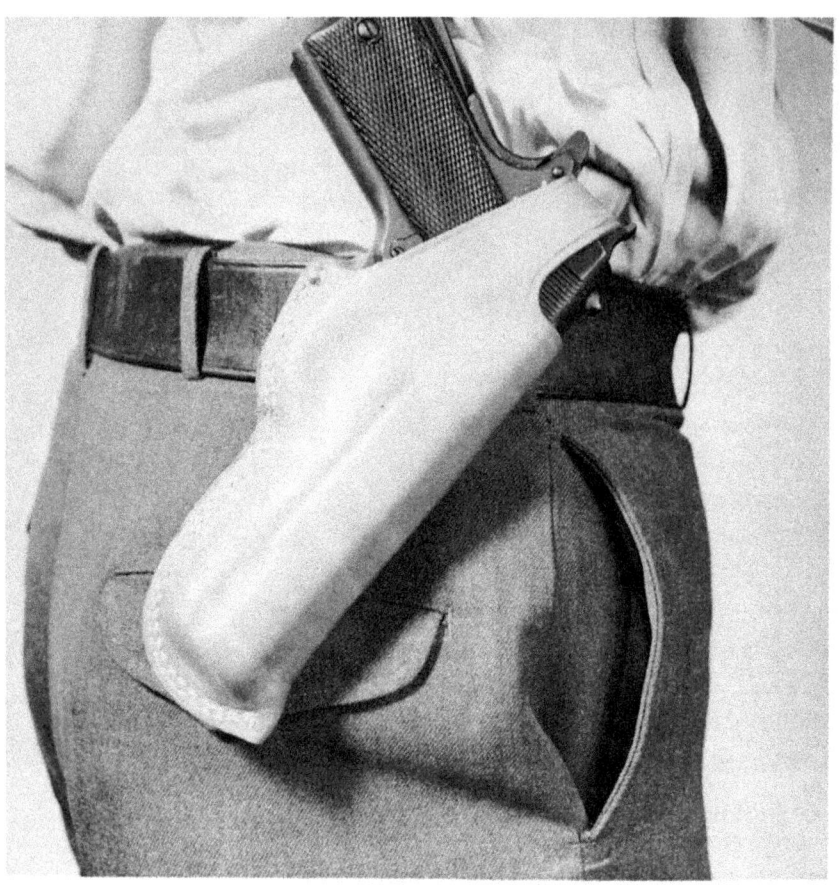

Commando holster for the Colt Government Model .45. This holster is designed to meet the needs of the modern armed forces.

our servicemen deserve something better than a holster designed for service with Jeb Stuart. Many servicemen having varied types of duty are required to carry sidearms. Many of these men are not carrying firearms, in direct violation of orders, simply because to do so would jeopardize their lives. A proper holster for service use would be a high-riding scabbard, worn on the right side, directly under the arm, fitting snugly against the body, and having a safe but fast retaining strap securing the gun in the holster. A holster of this type would allow the wearer to crawl through narrow openings, barb wire, and dense brush without the danger that the holster would get fouled. We can only hope that before long the thinking in the Pentagon will result in giving our men holsters that meet the problems of today, not those of a century ago.

CHAPTER 12

Field Holsters

A FIELD HOLSTER must be comfortable to wear during the long hours afield. Second, it must afford protection for the gun. It should have a retaining strap to keep the gun from dropping out in a fall. If the handgun is the primary weapon, it is best holstered on the right side of the body. If the handgun is your secondary weapon, the cross draw is best, because if the gun were carried on the right side, it would most certainly scar the stocks of both your rifle and handgun. If a gun has a barrel longer than six inches, it is advisable to carry the gun in a high, very tilted cross-draw scabbard, or a Dragoon Holster.

Almost all field holsters made have a very large belt loop that would require a belt three or four inches wide to fit it snugly, believe it or not. For greatest comfort, a field holster should fit snugly on a one-and-three-quarter-inch belt. The same thing is true of field holsters as of service holsters: if the gun is held rigid on a snug-fitting belt, you will not be conscious of the weight — even with the heaviest of the big magnums.

Although the fast-draw factor is not so important with this type of holster, it can be very important in big-game country. I do not like a flap holster for any use, and certainly not under field conditions. The large flap is too easily opened while going through brush, and in a slide down a hill or mountainside you are all too liable to lose your gun.

For a single-action gun I prefer a Skintite Holster on my right side or a high cross-draw scabbard on my left side. There is no need for a retaining

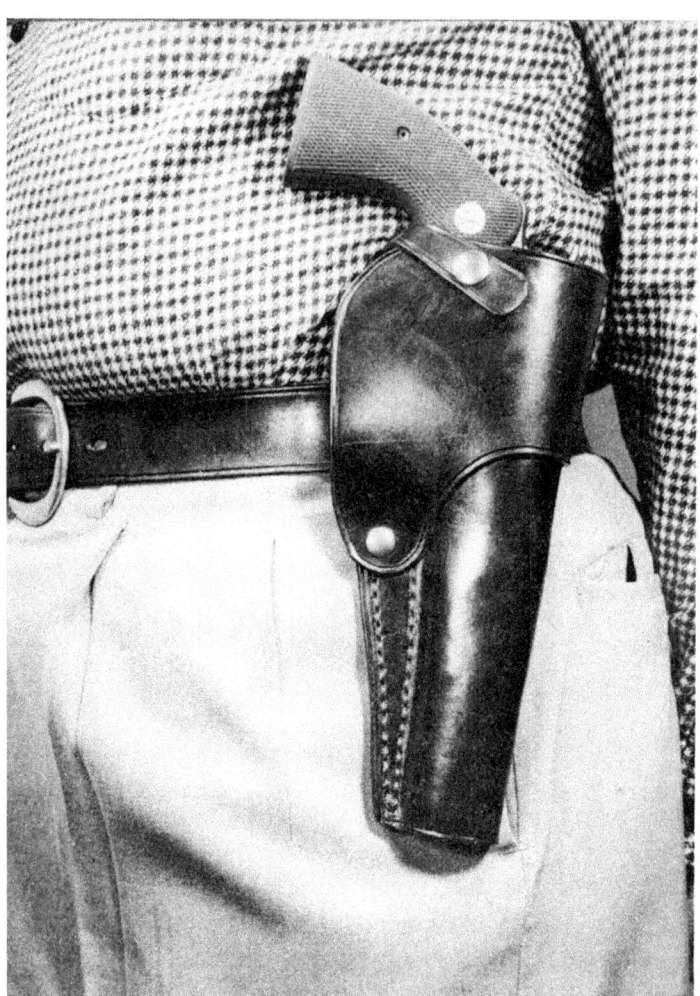 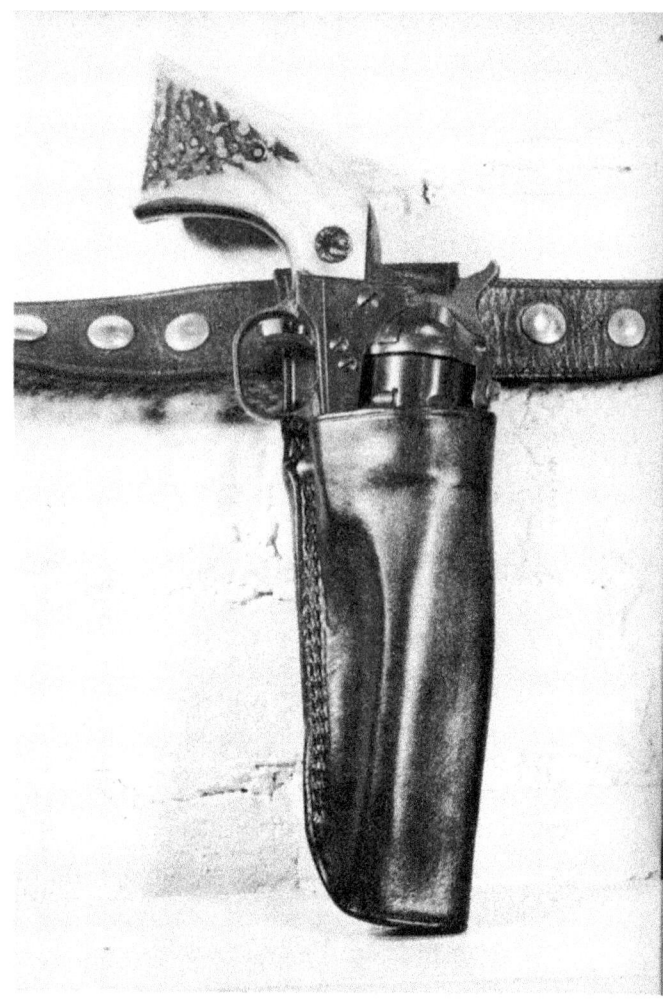

(Left) Dragoon holster — One of the most satisfactory field holsters for long-barrel revolvers. *(Right)* Missouri Skintite holster shown with a Ruger Single Six.

strap on these holsters, as they can be fitted so tightly that they will retain the gun under all circumstances.

Many people, when buying a field holster, choose the thickest, bulkiest one they can find and figure they are getting their money's worth. Then they discover that they can't sit down comfortably with it and that it is constantly shifting around as they walk. No wonder they're so tired after a day in the field!

Several years ago I made a gift of a holster to a well-known gun expert, editor, and writer, who told me that he had never liked to carry a handgun in the field. After one day of wearing my rig he told me he wouldn't have believed that toting a gun could be so comfortable. Since that time he has become a rabid handgunner and does at least half of his hunting with one hand.

CHAPTER 13

Western Holsters

THE SINGLE-ACTION revolver has been a favorite in this country since frontier days. The fact that a Single-Action Colt today costs ten times what it did when it was an absolute necessity doesn't deter anyone. Bill Ruger has improved upon Sam Colt's original designs so that they are among the finest field guns obtainable.

There is a definite swing to the very long-barreled Buntline Single-Actions for field use. This king-size cannon can be a headache to the person who has to holster it, but its superb accuracy makes it well worth the trouble. There are only three practical holsters for these "Long Toms" of the handgun world. The best, in my opinion, is a high cavalry-draw scabbard. With this holster worn far back over the right hip, the gun can be drawn, cocked, aimed, and fired with amazing speed. It is a superb holster for field use when the handgun is the primary weapon.

My second choice is a high-angled cross-draw scabbard. This holster is almost as fast as the cavalry draw. It is very comfortable and can be carried easily with a rifle.

So can my third choice — the Dragoon holster. The Dragoon holster is extremely comfortable and carries the gun as though it were in a shoulder holster. It is a very fast holster for such a long-barreled gun.

All three of these holsters are ideal for single-action guns having barrels longer than six and a half inches. This is true whether the gun to be holstered is a Single Six .22 Magnum, a Super Blackhawk .44 Magnum, or a Colt Buntline. For field use with a single-action, I recommend the Missouri Skintite. The Ringo cross draw is the most satisfactory cross-draw rig.

Jess Dodge demonstrates a Gun Hawk single-action rig, showing the proper backward cant of the holster for a fast single-action draw.

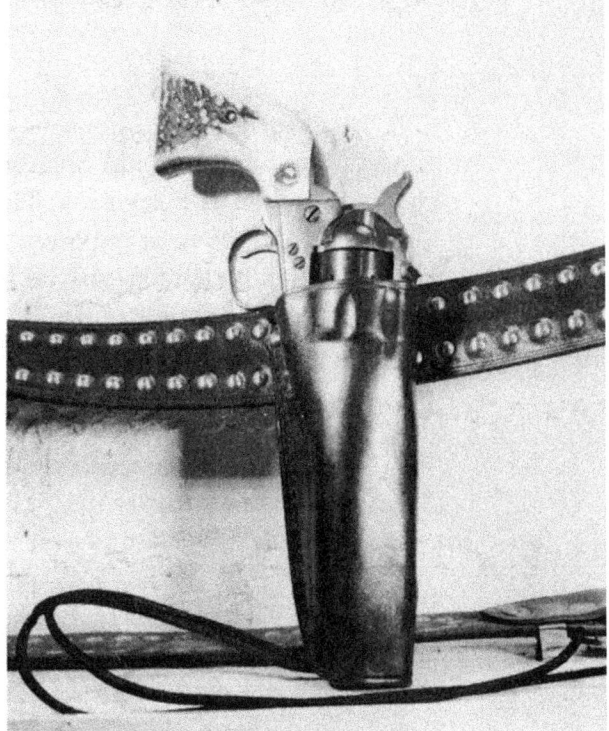

(Left) Cavalry Draw holster shown with the Ruger Single Six.

(Right) Outlaw holster with a Ruger Single Six.

For quick-draw work with any gun having a barrel longer than four and three-quarter inches, the cavalry-draw holster is, in my opinion, the fastest possible. This draw takes longer to learn but, once mastered, is so much faster that there is no comparison.

In the past few years the TV horse operas have sparked a nationwide interest in the fast draw. Contests are held throughout the nation. Electronic timers are used to establish the winners. Unfortunately, some shooters are doing fast-draw work with live ammo. This is extremely dangerous and should be attempted only by experts of long standing. Wax bullets and blank cartridges are all that should be used.

For fast-draw work a single-action gun should have the four-and-three-quarter-inch barrel. The less barrel you have to pull out of the holster, the faster your draw will be. Lightweight guns are not good for fast-draw work. The weight and balance of the all-steel single-actions are an advantage.

To be satisfactory for fast-draw work a holster must fit the gun snugly, fit the belt snugly, and have a good tie-down. When the gun is holstered, the holster and belt should be held so rigidly in place that there is absolutely no horizontal or vertical movement. This insures that the gun is held in the identical position for each draw.

There should be nothing impeding your hand as it grasps the gun, no matter from what direction you start. This means no wide, ornate buscadero belt, and no flopping long loops that jiggle through the slots of the belts.

The holster should be as sleek, fast, and uncluttered as a puma and as immovable as Pikes Peak. The gun butt should ride between wrist and elbow. One of the most important factors in the design of a fast-draw rig for single-action is that the gun be held with the butt canted *backward* to a marked degree. Every commercial "fast-draw" holster made today is pitched at the wrong angle. They violate every basic rule for fast draw.

Many such holsters are built so that the gun is cocked in the holster. This is great for promoting the sale of Unguentine and surgical braces. When handling the old knuckle-duster, you should always bear in mind that this gun, with its total absence of any safety factors, has shot more men accidentally than it ever did on purpose.

The time-honored, proven, and tested Outlaw or Half-breed holster of the Kansas-Missouri border fame, when worn on a heavy slanted one-and-three-quarter-inch belt and tied down with a thong, is the most economical and one of the best rigs for fast-draw practice.

There are on the market expensive super-fast rigs with steel-reinforced drop shanks. They have strap and buckle tie downs that are made especially for super-fast draw work. You should not contemplate buying one of these rigs until you can draw and fire in two-fifths of a second.

A fast-draw holster should be slick on the inside, either boned or lined with heavy top-grain cowhide. The fastest holster of all is the one lined with heavy industrial sharkskin. This is the hardest leather known: it resists scuffing and abrasion and presents a fast, friction-free surface for the draw. Wes Hardin or Ben Thompson would have put their grandmothers in hock to have had high-speed rigs like these.

CHAPTER 14

Commercial Targets

THERE ARE very few good silhouette targets available to the shooting public. Colt has one that is used by many police departments for combat shooting. However, it is sold only in large quantities so it is tough to come by for the average shooter interested in combat shooting or for members of small-town police departments. Many big-city departments are either unwilling or unable to give combat training to men in their department. A disadvantage of the Colt silhouette target is that it is not a full-figure outline but only a head and torso. The target nearly fills the paper on which it is printed, which results in shooters aiming at the paper rather than at the silhouetted figure. The ideal combat target would be a life-sized silhouette of a man in a menacing attitude centered on a piece of paper the size of a bed sheet. This would force the combat shooter to shoot at the outlined figure and not at the general area of the paper. The Stoeger Arms Corporation (45-18 Court Square, Long Island City 1, New York) has a police training target that is reasonably good for combat training — but, again, it is not a full figure.

A few years ago I designed two combat targets that, when tested, proved very effective for training in double-action shooting. The full-figure targets, printed in black on an orange-yellow background, were designed to be fired at from a distance of five yards. The figure was scaled to represent a six-foot man at twenty yards. These targets turned out to be very effective ego deflators. Men who thought themselves infallible on the Colt target at seven yards found it very difficult to get more than one or two hits anywhere on this target, which was six feet closer.

One practical method of testing your combat accuracy is to take a standard 50-yard pistol target and to reverse it in the holder so that you are shooting at the blank reverse side of the target. Then try to place as many shots as possible in the center of the blank paper. By scoring your hits on the printed side of the target, you can see just where and how you are grouping your shots.

IMPROVISED TARGETS

The scarcity of good available commercial combat targets has led to improvising combat targets that are far more effective than their commercial counterparts. A dummy, made by stuffing an old pair of coveralls with rags, swinging on the end of a rope tied to an overhead tree branch is a lot more fun to shoot at than any printed target. The same dummy sliding down a slanted overhead wire across your line of fire is a lot tougher to hit than a stationary target. A large cardboard disk fitted inside an old automobile tire with an eight-inch bull's-eye painted in the center is extremely hard to hit as it rolls and bounces down the hillside across your line of fire. If you succeed in putting just one shot in a bull's-eye on this target, you are doing well. Many appliance manufacturers furnish their dealers with large life-sized lithograph cutouts to be used in their display rooms. By cultivating your local appliance dealer you can usually persuade him to give you these cutouts when he is through with them. They make excellent targets. With a coping saw and a little ingenuity, very good targets can be cut out of scrap plywood, beaverboard, masonite, and even from a wide plank. When manipulated with wires, these targets can be made to pop out from behind trees, bushes, or just pop up from the ground.

You can settle the arguments as to who is the "top gun" in any group of combat shooters by using a very simple and easily made target that will provide hours of fun and good combat training. All that is needed to make this target is a six-foot length of two-by-six, a six-foot length of two-by-four, an eight- or ten-inch lag bolt, and two one-foot lengths of two-by-twelve planking. The two-by-six piece is pointed at one end and driven into the ground to a depth of about two feet with the narrow edge of the board facing the firing line. A hole is bored downward in the top of the two-by-six. The lag belt is screwed into this hole, which should be slightly less in diameter than the thread diameter of the lag bolt. The head of the lag bolt is then sawed off with a hack saw and the top of the shank of the lag bolt

Photo by Martin Doll

Combat practice is fun — the other fellow's misses can provide more laughs than your hits.

filed smooth, with the edges slightly rounded. A hole somewhat larger than the diameter of the protruding shank of the lag bolt should be drilled at right angles in the narrow edge of the two-by-four, to a depth of about three inches. The two-by-four is placed on the protruding lag bolt, with about a half-inch clearance between the two-by-four crossbeam and the top of the two-by-six post. Axle grease placed in the hole in the two-by-four allows it to pivot freely on the exposed shank of the lag bolt. The twelve-inch two-by-twelve blocks are nailed to the broad side of the two-by-four, one at each end of the two-by-four beam. The large wooden blocks are painted white.

The finished target is somewhat like a child's seesaw turned sideways. A slight pressure at one end of the crosspiece will cause it to pivot easily. Two contestants stand on the firing line, each facing his end of the target, which should be parallel to the firing line. At a given signal each draws and fires at the wooden block at his end of the beam. The first man to hit target

Commercial Targets   97

will of course knock his target backward, swinging his opponent's target out of the line of fire. Both contestants should use the same caliber weapon if possible; otherwise, if they score hits at exactly the same time, the one with the heavier-caliber gun would win because his bullet would exert more force on his end of the beam than would the lighter-caliber one striking the other end. This is a game in which both speed and accuracy count.

One of the best methods of improving your double-action shooting is by banging away at aerial targets. Most shooters have blazed away at aerial targets at some time in their shooting career and have given it up as a bad bargain. The trouble, generally, has been that they begin by shooting at targets too difficult for them. The beginner should start out by shooting at one-gallon tin cans, thrown into the air so that they fall relatively near to him. He should continue to fire at this size target until he can consistently hit it nine out of ten times. He should then switch to a slightly smaller-sized tin can. By gradually reducing the size of the can at which he is shooting he can become an expert shot in a relatively short period of time. I have known shooters who started out with one-gallon cans and in six months were able to shoot through the center of one-and-three-quarter-inch washers tossed in the air. The hole in the center of the washer is five-eighths of an inch in diameter; and any man who can do shooting like that would be mighty stiff competition in a gun fight.

CHAPTER 15

Safe Gun Handling

THE MOST DANGEROUS thing about today's handgun is the person who is using it. Accidents involving firearms don't happen — they are caused. All gun accidents could be prevented if shooters would develop and abide by a set of safe gun-handling habits. The proof of this fact is that well-organized target ranges where safety rules are rigidly enforced by range officers are far safer places in which to spend your time than your own home. Accidents on properly run ranges are as rare as the dodo bird.

The most important rule for firearm safety is never to point any weapon, whether it is loaded or unloaded, at anything or anyone that you don't want to kill. The second commandment of gun safety is to make sure that your handgun is in safe operating condition. Have your gun checked periodically by a competent gunsmith. If your weapon is in A-1 condition, the only thing you have to worry about is yourself.

Never try to clean or work on a loaded firearm. It will take you much less time to remove the cartridges from the gun than it will take a surgeon to remove a bullet from your carcass. Revolvers can be handled by the average person with a far greater degree of safety than can the semi-automatic pistol. I have seen many accidents or near accidents involving semi-automatic pistols but I have never seen one involving a revolver. If I had a dollar for every time I've been handed an "empty" semi-automatic pistol with the clip removed — only to find upon checking the weapon that the cartridge had been left in the chamber — I would be a far richer man than I am today. Semi-automatic pistols should be checked to make sure they are not loaded — and then double-checked.

I have heard of accidental shootings with revolvers, but upon investigation I discovered that the cause of the accident was a malfunction not of the weapon but of the person holding the gun. When unloading a revolver it is wise first to count the cartridges you have removed from the gun and then to look through the chambers in the cylinder to make sure that you have not left a round in the gun. Some Smith & Wesson revolvers are apt to retain a cartridge in the chamber nearest to the frame if the crane holding the cylinder is not allowed to swing fully open.

Never attempt to spin or juggle a loaded gun unless you are tired of living. If your urge to ape the Lone Ranger is uncontrollable, at least make doubly sure that the equalizer you are misusing is beyond a doubt unloaded. Never attempt to practice extreme fast draw with a gun loaded with live ammunition. Blank cartridges or wax bullets are all that should be used. Only after your speed, accuracy, and control of the weapon have become infallible with wax bullets should you ever consider working with live ammo.

Never have your finger inside the trigger guard when you are holstering the gun. Not a few people have accidentally shot themselves or someone else by failing to observe this rule. It is also wise to keep your forefinger clear of the trigger guard when you are drawing your weapon. Observance of this rule does *not* slow your quick-draw time. For several years I believed that I had my trigger finger inside the guard as I drew and fired while doing exhibition fast-draw work from a very speedy cut-down hip scabbard. But a series of ultra-fast photographs taken by a high-speed camera showed that my finger did not enter the trigger guard until the gun was clear of the holster and well on the way out in front of me toward the firing position. The total elapsed time of my draw from that holster was one-fifth of a second from the starting signal until the weapon was fired.

Holster malfunction is a major cause of gun accidents. It is common sense for you to ascertain whether the holster you are wearing is safe both for the day-in-and-day-out packing of your pistol and also for use under the stress of an emergency.

To make certain that your gun is safely holstered for everyday use, first unload your gun, then check to see whether the gun can be cocked while still inside the holster. If the cylinder will turn without use of undue force inside your holster, you'd better throw it away and get a holster that properly fits the gun. If your holster has no retaining device, hold the holster upside down over a bed or cushion and see if the gun remains in your scabbard. A properly fitted scabbard should retain the gun in an upside-down position even when shaken lightly. If your scabbard will not pass this test, then it is either improperly fitted or is too worn to retain the gun safely.

"Gimmick holsters" featuring button releases which must be pressed with the trigger finger through the trigger guard are as sure a way of inviting the undertaker as any I know of. A holster of this type is worn by about 30 per cent of the men on one of the world's largest police forces. They buy this holster because the official holster of this department is even more unsafe. Each year about a dozen of these officers shoot themselves while trying to draw their weapons. Long retaining straps that pass over the hammer or behind the trigger guard of a revolver are apt to become fouled when drawing a gun in an emergency. This constitutes a serious hazard with a double-action revolver.

Never take chances with ammunition that you are not thoroughly familiar with. Just because the cartridge will fit into your gun does not necessarily mean that it is a safe load for your weapon. A "hot" hand load intended for use on a Colt New Service .38 or Smith & Wesson Outdoorsman could turn an air-weight Chief Special or a Colt Cobra into a close approximation of a hand grenade with the ring pin pulled.

When plinking or target shooting, make sure that you are shooting against a safe backstop. When hunting with a handgun, clearly identify your game before you shoot. *Never shoot at a rustle in the bushes.* Never forget that your gun is a lethal weapon. Always handle it in the presence of others as you would want them to handle their weapons around you.

CHAPTER 16

Close Combat Shooting

THE MAJORITY of gun fights occur at very close quarters and in small areas — that seem even smaller while the shooting is going on. FBI combat training is based on the premise that the agents will be shooting it out with felons at distances of twenty feet or less.

The most famous gun fight in history, when the Earp brothers, together with gambler Doc Holliday, blasted the Clantons and McLowerys occurred in the O. K. Corral, a small space between a couple of buildings, just about the size of a croquet court. This gun fight was over in less than a minute, according to eyewitness reports at the time, and although shotguns as well as six-guns were employed by the Earp factions, some of their intended victims escaped and the cowboy faction succeeded in wounding one of the Earps. If modern close-combat gun-fighting techniques had been used, the slaughter would have been more widespread and over in about half the time.

Special agents of the United States Treasury Department, Bureau of Narcotics, must be able to draw their weapons and fire five shots into the kill area of a man-sized silhouette target at seven yards in less than three seconds in order to meet that agency's rigid standards. A properly trained man should be able to draw and fire a killing shot at a felon at a distance of seven yards or less in no more than one half a second, including recognition time. Shooting done under these conditions will of necessity be fired double-action. Combat shooting bears the same relationship to target shooting that judo does to ballet. The main objective in a close-quarter gun fight is to put your enemy out of action in the shortest possible time. The best weapons for this sort of work are submachine guns or riot guns, but since such emergencies don't allow you the time to go home and get one, it's advisable to know how to do effective work with your handgun.

If your weapon is a .44 Magnum, a Colt .45 or .44 Special, you have a tremendous edge in this form of combat because with these weapons a hit almost anywhere on your opponent's carcass will put him out of action. A .357 Magnum also does a workmanlike job. Nothing smaller than a .38 Special should even be considered as a combat weapon.

Across-the-body draws are a definite hazard for fast combat work. The ideal combat draw is from the hip on the side of the shooting hand. Surveys made at the scenes of countless shootings show that the tendency among both trained and untrained shooters is to shoot high and to the shooter's left of the person they are shooting at. This is true of the right-handed man; a left-hander is inclined to shoot high and to his right. For this reason it is wise to crouch forward and step to your left when drawing the gun.

The percentages are with you that your adversary's first shot will miss you. Upon drawing your weapon, whip it out in front of you where you can see and control the direction in which it is pointed. In too many cases a hastily triggered shot from the hip will plow through the ground or floor in front of you. If you have practiced this maneuver with silhouette targets, the percentages are again that you will drop your man with your first shot.

Immediately after firing your first shot, squat lower, balancing on the balls of your feet, cup the palm of your left hand under the butt of your revolver, and bring both elbows in, pressing tightly to your sides. In this way your gun is firmly held in both hands pointing straight ahead of the center of your body. Hold your head pointed directly ahead and pivot your body at your adversary or adversaries. When you are facing your enemy, fire double-action. Bullets fired from your gun in this fashion should strike your adversary in the pelvic area. There are many large, heavy bones in this general area. When a bullet strikes these heavy bones and shatters them, the impact and shock will put him out of action. A bullet hitting the fluids in the intestine imparts a high degree of hydrostatic shock. A bullet hitting the pelvis anywhere near the spine imparts a paralyzing shock to the spinal column.

I have known of many cases of men hit in and around the heart by .38-caliber bullets who continued to shoot it out until they fell dead. Use of the close-combat technique just described will insure more hits in less time and with greater personal safety than any other method of close-quarter gun fighting.

No. 1 — *(left)* Punching out your first shot from a fast draw.
No. 2 — *(right)* Center braced crouch.

If the terrain in which the gun fight occurs rules out the use of the close-combat technique because of obstructions, then, if possible, you should turn those obstructions to your advantage. It is wise to take cover in a gun fight whenever possible. Then the obstruction may be used both as a barricade and as a rest to steady your shooting hand. In a street gun fight at close quarters, many a police officer has saved his life by throwing himself sprawling in the gutter and firing from the slight but effective protection of the curb. In this manner he presents a much smaller target to his enemy. Fire hydrants, lampposts, mailboxes, and fire-alarm boxes provide excellent cover for combat even though the government agencies involved take a dim view of having their equipment riddled with bullets. I know of one such gun fight that touched off a veritable crossfire of memos between the department of sanitation and the police department of a large metropolitan city. A detective shooting it out with a bandit had ducked behind a heavy metal trash receptacle. The officer shot and killed the felon, who had emptied his gun into the trash can in a vain attempt to hit the sleuth. In my opinion the trash can was only serving its purpose in keeping our city streets clean. Contrary to general belief, police officers bleed when wounded just like everybody else!

There are several other versions of close-combat techniques in current use. Each one has something in its favor and all of them are considerably

Side-hip shooting braced.

better than the total absence of any planned program for defensive shooting. Some federal agencies train their men to shoot from a crouch with the elbow of the shooting arm pressed hard against the side of the body at waist level. This is a very good combat style granted there's an unlimited supply of ammunition available for use in practicing this technique. However, in my opinion, there is a much greater area of miscalculation when the gun is held at the side of the body than when it is centered directly in front of the shooter's torso. Another group of federal men are trained to shoot from a crouch with the elbow braced against the body and the wrist of the shooting hand supported by the free hand. This is, I believe, superior to the other federal method but it has more drawbacks than the technique described earlier. Minor variations of this method have the free hand braced on either knee.

Some instructors with the New York City Police Department favor shooting from a squatting position with the shooting hand held straight out from the body at shoulder height. This technique, good in theory, in practice proves to be too cramped and unbalanced a position from which to shoot both fast and accurately. Many old-time gun fighters have claimed that poking or punching the gun at their intended victim as they fired double-action improved their shooting in a fast gun fight. I tried shooting at silhouette targets in this fashion myself and found it to be extremely effective but not quite so sure-fire as the techniques advocated at the beginning of this chapter. It was possible to score a large percentage of hits but they were not so well centered on the target as the rapid groups in one or more silhouette targets using my method. The only variations in the grouping were up and down in the center of the target with little or no variation in the horizontal spacing of shots.

Gun fights are not fought according to a set of rules. Never give a hoodlum a break. Always bear in mind that if you give him a chance to shoot you in the back he'll go out of his way to accommodate you. As one old western peace officer told me when reminiscing about the old days, "When it came to gun talk I was meaner than a she-grizzly guarding her cubs but I was toting a badge and had the law on my side."

Police shoulder point

CHAPTER 17

Alley Cleaning

ALLEY CLEANING is the technique of gun fighting to be used in close-quarters combat in total darkness or in semi-darkness, where you and your adversary cannot see, or have extreme difficulty in seeing, one another.

The best weapon for this sort of work is Colt's .45-caliber Government Model automatic. Its heavy caliber, rapid rate of fire, and the speed with which it can be loaded in the dark make it an ideal weapon for this sort of work.

Alley cleaning is the one type of gun fighting in which you hope your adversary will fire first, since you need the flash of his weapon to show you his position. You then bracket that area with a very rapid barrage of shots, during and after which you change your own location and position as rapidly and quietly as possible. In most cases, if you have spaced your shots properly you will have hit your adversary with your first burst. If not, you should reload and wait for him to shoot again. Shooting in the dark is at best a very difficult thing to do, aimed shots being impossible. You must rely on instinctive shooting.

I know of only one police department that gives its men any training at all in this kind of shooting. They take their men to a totally dark pistol range. They have about a dozen silhouette targets placed around the range. At the base of each target is a small but very bright spotlight pointed upward at the target. These lights are controlled by a man behind the firing squad. He flicks various lights on one at a time for a fraction of a second.

The officer on the firing line fires at the target from memory of its location. After a few times at bat the men develop an amazing skill in instinctive shooting, many of them doing almost as well in total darkness as they do in their daylight combat practice. This same group also receives instruction in firing at sound in total darkness. Buzzers are attached at the base of these targets and activated for short periods. After considerable practice, the men become skilled enough to place a shot within a two-foot radius of the source of the sound.

According to FBI figures, 80 per cent of all gun fights between criminals and peace officers occur after dark, and yet not one police department in a thousand does anything to train its men for combat under these prevailing conditions. If it has any firearms-training program at all, it consists of formal target shooting on brightly lit ranges, which is a pleasant pastime but doesn't equip a man to defend himself in a gun fight.

CHAPTER 18

Mid-Range Combat

FREQUENTLY peace officers become involved in gun fights with felons at ranges greater than the seven-yards distance to which close-combat techniques apply. These greater distances require different combat techniques. The ones following have been found effective at ranges of from ten to sixty yards.

Many police departments favor the standard stance used in formal target shooting — that is, with the shooting arm extended at shoulder height and the free hand either relaxed at the side or clasping the belt or in the side pants pocket. This is a very relaxed position from which to shoot at paper targets, which are not shooting back. However, in a gun fight few people have either the ability or the inclination to relax. Furthermore, shootings at these ranges more often than not follow either a tussle or a chase and frequently both of these disturbing factors have preceded the shooting. Foot racing and hand-to-hand combat have never been noted for their tranquilizing effect upon the human nervous system. After such stimuli a police officer firing at a felon from this "relaxed" stance would have difficulty hitting a bull in the behind with a baseball bat, let alone score a decisive hit on a fast-moving hoodlum with a handgun! A handgun held at arm's length under these conditions would be wiggling around like Little Egypt on a carnival midway.

Simple logic tells us that for firing under these conditions the gun should be supported as rigidly as possible. In open terrain, where no cover

Rock the Baby

is available to duck behind and upon which to rest the shooting hand, the "rock-the-baby" hold is the most effective possible way to fire a gun in open terrain mid-range combat. The rock-the-baby hold is so simple and easy to use that tremendous increases in accuracy can be noted from the very first and it takes very little practice to become a veritable Dead-Eye Dick. Many police officers who learned this technique in combat practice like it so well that they now use this method while hunting with their handguns. One-shot kills on deer with .357 Magnums have become the rule rather than the exception with these men.

To use the "rock-the-baby" hold (assuming that the shooter is right-handed) the revolver is held in the right hand, with the heel of the right hand and the bottom of the gun butt resting on the elbow joint of the left arm, while the palm of the left hand is cupped around the right elbow. Both arms are raised to shoulder height in this fashion. From this very steady rest the revolver is cocked and fired single-action. The gun is raised or lowered by raising or lowering both arms in unison. Horizontal changes are accomplished by pivoting the upper part of the body to the right or left in the direction desired.

On a picnic a year ago a bunch of policemen plinking at beer cans were

Braced shoulder level

holding their guns in this fashion. One of the patrolmen's wives, who had never fired a gun before in her life, thought that it looked like a lot of fun. Amid a lot of heckling she held her husband's Colt Official Police in this fashion and popped away at the beer cans, some fifty yards away. She drilled six cans with six shots and remarked as she finished that it was too easy. They kept putting the cans farther and farther away; she kept on hitting them, and was still drilling nice round holes in the cans at one hundred and ten paces when they ran out of ammunition. It was quite an exhibition of marksmanship for a novice, especially in view of the fact that she was more than seven months pregnant.

The Army worked out a reasonably effective method for mid-range combat. In this method the gun is grasped in the right hand and the left hand clasped firmly around the right hand. Both arms are extended at shoulder height, the pistol being centered directly in front of the body. The gun is fired single- or double-action, with horizontal changes in the point of aim being accomplished by pivoting the body. This method is far superior to one-handed shooting, but it gives results not quite so accurate as the rock-the-baby hold.

If there is cover available, such as fences, doorways, large mailboxes,

Barricade shooting around corner

or automobiles, you'll be extremely foolish not to take advantage of them in any gun fight at any range. Shooting from behind a barricade is an entirely different technique. In almost every case shooting from behind a barricade should be done single-action, that is the revolver should be cocked, aimed, and fired. Firearms training with progressive police departments places a great deal of emphasis on this type of shooting.

The well-trained police officer should be equally effective when firing his weapon from behind a barricade with either right or left hand. This is very important, because a police officer may find himself crouched in a doorway or a fence so situated as to afford protection for his body only if he is shooting with his left hand. When firing from a barricade with the right hand, greater accuracy will be achieved if the gun is resting in the webbing between the thumb and forefinger of the left hand, which is braced against the barricade. The reverse would be true when shooting left-handed. When it is possible to shoot either right-handed or left-handed behind a barricade, it is wise to vary the side of the barricade from which you are shooting so that your adversary cannot anticipate the place from which your next shot will be fired. Otherwise, all he has to do is train his gun on the spot where you are repeatedly exposing yourself.

If the cover from which you are shooting is a door or wooden fence that obscures your adversary's view of you but does not stop his bullets from drilling through, it is wise to present as small a target for chance bullets as possible. Even if the fence is seven feet high it's foolhardy to stand erect behind such cover. It's better to kneel and crouch low or, still better, to lie prone on the ground. In this fashion you reduce the chances of your being hit by a blind shot through your cover.

It is definitely to your advantage if you can identify the type of weapon with which your adversary is armed. Cover that affords you complete protection if he is armed with a .32 or a snub-nosed .38 is totally inadequate if he is armed with a heavy-caliber revolver, a .9-millimeter Luger, a Browning High-power, or a Colt Super .38 or .45 Automatic. If he is armed with any of the many 7.65-millimeter or .380-caliber foreign automatics or a snub-nosed .38, and your service pistol is a four- or six-inch barreled .38 loaded with high-speed cartridges or Magnums, your best tactic would be to fall back a few yards out of his range and drop him with one well-aimed shot in comparative safety. Small foreign automatics and snub-nosed .38's are extremely inaccurate at ranges beyond 60 yards, and at 100 yards a bow and arrow would be better. On the other hand, accurate shooting at 200 yards is possible with a good service revolver. The great Ed McGivern proved that an expert handgunner armed with a Smith & Wesson .357 Magnum with an eight-and-three-eighth-inch barrel could score repeated killing shots on a man-sized target at 600 yards — which is darn good rifle shooting for a handgunner!

(Left) Back braced . . .

(Right) Border Patrol method

CHAPTER 19

Long-Range Shooting

A GOOD REVOLVER is capable of far greater accuracy than is the human being who will shoot it. Very accurate shots can be made consistently at ranges of from 100 to 300 yards by use of several techniques especially devised for long-distance shooting. The heavy-frame .38-caliber revolvers that have four-inch barrels and are capable of safely handling "hot" loads can place shots accurately up to 200 yards, depending upon the ammunition used. The .357 Magnum and .44 Magnum revolvers having barrels six inches in length or longer can be extremely effective at nearly twice that range. The .44-40 and .44 Special revolvers that can handle beefed-up hand loads are also capable of extremely effective long-range shots.

The United States Border Patrol has developed a very effective method of long-distance shooting. A right-handed shooter kneels on his right knee, placing his left foot firmly on the ground in a comfortable position. The left elbow is placed on the left knee with the forearm raised in an upward position. The gun held in the right hand is rested on the palm of the left. The revolver is cocked, aimed, and fired single-action. It is a very steady position, one from which it is possible to hit a man at 200 yards.

Very well-aimed shots can be fired at long range by leaning with the forearm resting across the hood of an automobile. The gun in this case is held firmly with both hands and fired single-action. The best method for precision shooting at extremely long ranges is to sit on the ground with your back braced against a tree, rock, or parked automobile. Your knees are drawn up in a comfortable position and the gun, held in both hands, is extended directly in front of you. With your knees pressed in against your extended forearm, the gun is then aimed and fired single-action. It was from this position that Ed McGivern riddled the middle of man-sized targets at 600 yards.

CHAPTER 20

Quick Draw*

A FAST DRAW depends on the ability to grasp a gun, pull it from its holster, bring it to bear on target, and fire it with telling effect in the shortest possible period of time. To do this you must eliminate all unnecessary motions. A fast draw should be accomplished with one continuous motion.

Too many fast-draw fans break up their draw into two separate motions. They first get a death grip on their guns and then they draw and fire. The gun should be picked up with an uninterrupted continuation of the motion begun when reaching for the weapon. The gun should be wiped into the hand and the shooting grip on the gun completed as you throw forward. The trigger squeeze should be coordinated so that the split second when the gun is in line with your target it fires.

Developing an extremely fast draw is hard physical work. Any additional strength you can develop in your fingers, wrist, and lower arm is a distinct advantage in double-action quick-draw. I have been told that every one of the old-time western gun fighters who were considered to be terribly dangerous had one thing in common — all had extremely powerful wrists and hands. I myself found that by the regular use of a spring grip exerciser I was able to whittle about one tenth of a second off my draw.

Too many men, in trying to develop a fast draw, choose a gun that is too cumbersome and heavy to manipulate with the great speed and dexterity necessary for super-fast gun handling.

* All photos in this chapter by David B. Eisendrath, Jr.

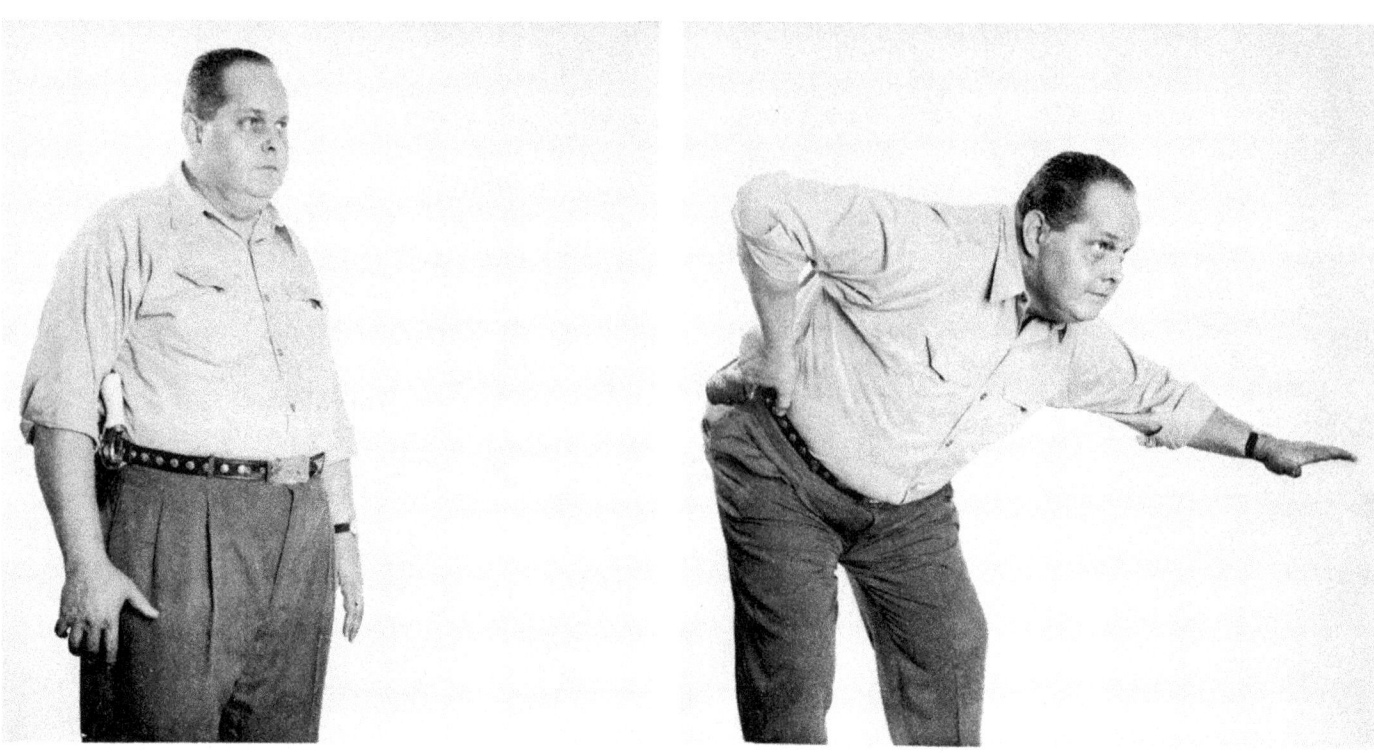

The FBI draw — one continuous movement. Note in picture 3 that the finger does not enter

I believe the long action of the Colt revolver perversely lends itself to fast-draw double-action work better than the more modern "short" action of the Smith & Wesson revolvers. However, the old long-action Smith & Wessons were the smoothest of all. Even though the actual lock time of the modern Smith & Wesson is less than that of the long-action guns, the trigger pull is too stiff, and overcoming inertia of the action at high speed is too time-consuming. The smoothness and effortlessness of firing the long-action revolvers are such that the only mechanical limitation to the speed of your draw is the speed with which you are able to pull the trigger.

If you are seriously interested in fast-draw work, regardless of the type of gun you are using, you will find that a few dollars spent in having your action honed and all bearing surfaces polished will be a sound investment in a faster draw.

Either by the use of custom grips or grip adapters, you should alter the grip of your gun so that no matter how fast you grab your weapon you will come up with a good shooting grip. The two most common shooting errors in fast draw are: grabbing the revolver too high on the grip so that the webbing of your hand interferes with the action of the hammer; and grasping the butt so low that all accuracy is lost and pulling the trigger is almost an impossibility.

Your holster is of paramount importance in fast-draw work, and it should hold your gun in such a manner that it is in perfect alignment with

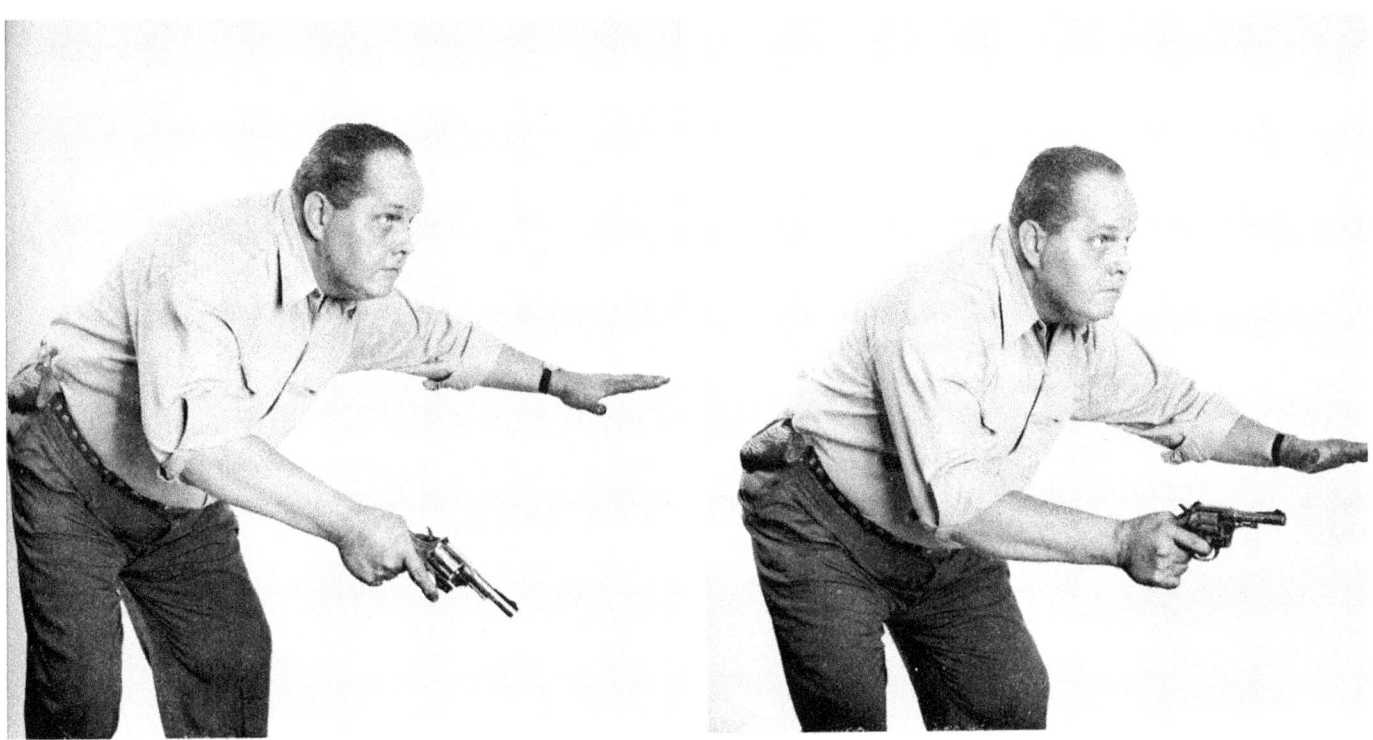

trigger guard until the gun is well toward firing position. The left hand is used to balance.

the direction of the motion used to bring it into firing position. The holster should be absolutely rigid with no side or up-and-down motion. There should be nothing in the construction of the holster to get in the way of your hand. Straps, buckles, conchos, or doodads on the body of the holster cause a slight hesitation as you slam your hand in. This should be true of any fast-draw holster, either modern or western.

The holster should be snug and hold the gun rigidly in exactly the same position each time you draw. A holster that has been boned on the inside or one that is lined with smooth, heavy top-grain cowhide is naturally faster. Messing up the inside of a holster with mixtures of vaseline, graphite, axle grease, or *paté de foie gras* results in nothing but a greasy, dirty gun.

All fast shooting should be done with either blank cartridges when going against an electronic timer, or wax bullets, when breaking balloons or shooting at combat targets. When handling guns at extremely high speed, there is no margin for error. Since accidents do happen, it is only common sense to take precautions and protect yourself — and protect your hobby from restrictive legislation.

Quick-Draw with Revolvers

FBI DRAW

The FBI draw is the most efficient and effective method of getting a revolver into action from a concealment holster. Its greatest advantage lies in the fact that no time is lost in bringing the weapon into firing position on the target. This is the only draw in which you can safely begin pulling the trigger while you are still bringing the gun into firing position. This fact gives you tremendous speed in combat shooting. You have more accuracy on your first shot with this draw, because of the throwing motion used.

Another advantage to this draw is the fact that it cannot be interfered with readily. It is more difficult for a hoodlum to stop in close-quarter tussle. Also, when using this type of draw you are crouched in a position that offers much less target area to your adversary.

ACROSS-THE-BODY DRAW

From a standpoint of speed and accuracy this method of draw is far less effective than any other method. The horizontal sweeping motion of the gun hand, with the consequent necessity of stopping and correcting this motion before shooting, is the problem. Devotees of this type of draw endeavor to prove their speed by demonstrations that always assume their adversary will be standing just to the left of their left shoulder. Unfortunately, this ideal condition seldom exists in actual combat.

Trooper Martin Spatz demonstrating the across-the-body draw. The left hip is rotated toward the gun hand and then quickly turned away as the gun is grasped, thus carrying the holster away from the weapon.

Drawing a gun from an ankle holster.

Photos courtesy of True — the Man's Magazine

ANKLE DRAW

This is the fastest possible draw from a sitting position whether in a car or seated in a chair. It is also effective when you are sent sprawling on the ground. Even from a normal standing position, it can be surprisingly fast. The ankle draw always carries with it a tremendous element of surprise.

SHOULDER DRAW

With a properly designed "directional draw" shoulder holster, a small revolver can be drawn and accurately fired with speed second only to the high hip draw. When used with an overcoat in the wintertime, it offers definite advantages over any other holster.

2 Methods of Clearing the Jacket

STEPPING THE COAT. This method of clearing the coat is the preferred method. The shooter bends forward and with his right foot in position takes a step to the left with his left foot. He knifes his coat aside with the edge of his hand as he reaches for his weapon. This has the advantage of getting the shooter low and to the left — out of his opponent's probable line of fire, which in most cases is high and to the shooter's right.

CLEARING THE COAT. This method is used when there is not room for the lunging step to the left necessary in "stepping the coat." It has the added advantage of confusing your adversary, whose attention is caught by the coat being raised by the left hand.

Trooper Martin Spatz with a shoulder rig. In drawing a weapon from a shoulder holster, the left shoulder is swung far to the right as the shooter bends into a combat crouch. This maneuver clears the coat and brings the gun toward the shooting hand. As the gun is grasped the left shoulder is rapidly turned away, helping to take the holster from the gun. Then with only a slight motion of the gun hand the weapon can be thrust into firing position.

QUICK DRAW WITH THE DRAGOON HOLSTER. The Dragoon is a combination field and service holster which enables a man to carry a handgun in a comfortable and effective manner. When the wearer is carrying a shoulder gun the handgun is out of the way.

It is recommended for police officers who must patrol alone in a car. It keeps the revolver on the opposite side of the body from any prisoner who might be taken into custody.

As you begin this draw the left hip is twisted to bring the holstered weapon towards the shooting hand. The hand passes by the holstered gun in a circular motion. On the return orbit of the hand, the spread fingers release the retaining strap and the gun butt drops into the hand, slanted in the direction of the draw. As you turn your hip, carrying the holster away from the gun, the weapon is rapidly brought into firing position.

HIGHWAY PATROL HOLSTER

The low right-hip draw is unquestionably the fastest method of drawing a long-barreled service revolver. The whole draw can be accomplished with one smooth, uninterrupted circular motion of the hand and arm.

Thumb in natural position disengages retaining strap.

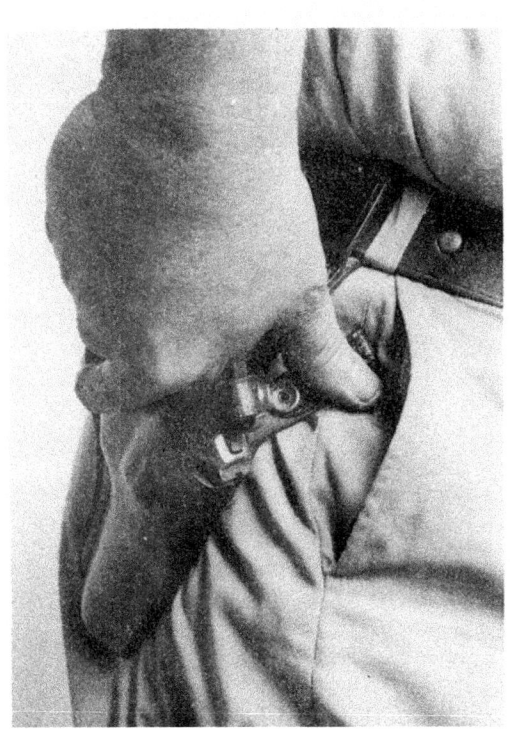

Fast Draw for Automatics

MEXICAN DEFENSE HOLSTER

Semi-automatic pistols were never designed to be used as fast-draw weapons. The pump priming before you can get it to gush is a little too time-consuming for quick draw. If it is carried ready to go it is in an unsafe condition. Its saw-handle construction throws roadblocks in the way of a smooth lightning draw. However, for those devotees of the auto pistol the draw from a tilted-across-the-body holster is the fastest. The inherent inaccuracies which accompany an across-the-body draw will scarcely be noticeable to one addicted to the use of these ammo burners.

FAST DRAW WITH THE MEXICAN DEFENSE HOLSTER

A DOUBLE-ACTION AUTOMATIC
DRAWN FROM A HIGH SCABBARD

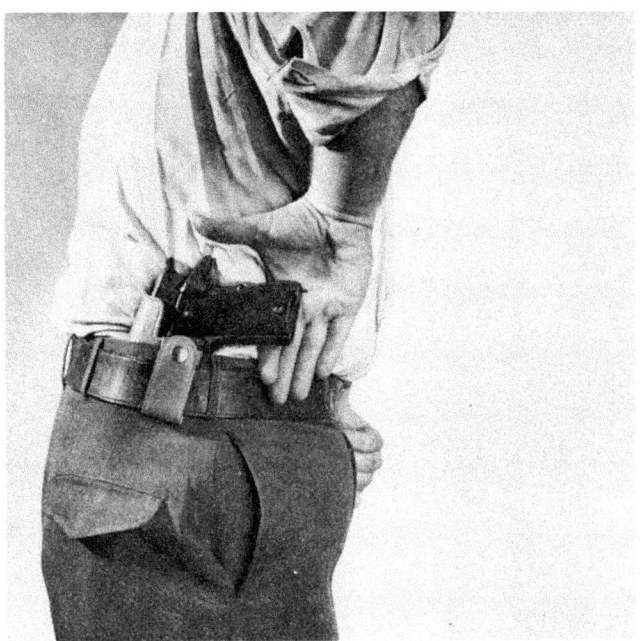 

(Top) As the hand twists in to grasp the gun, the thumb is placed on the hammer. *(Bottom)* As the gun is thrown forward and the elbow is snapped into the side, the weight of the weapon automatically cocks the hammer.

CAVALRY DRAW
WITH "INSIDE THE PANTS" HOLSTER

The cavalry draw from an "inside the pants" holster can be very fast for those who like to carry their pistol with a round in the chamber and the hammer down. The hammer is cocked as the pistol is thrown forward.

There is something very devil-may-care about the fellow who totes an automatic with a round in the chamber and goes in for quick draw. The Menninger Clinic has far more use for this type of shooter than have I or the Prudential Insurance Company, but in case you are interested, this is the way to go about it.

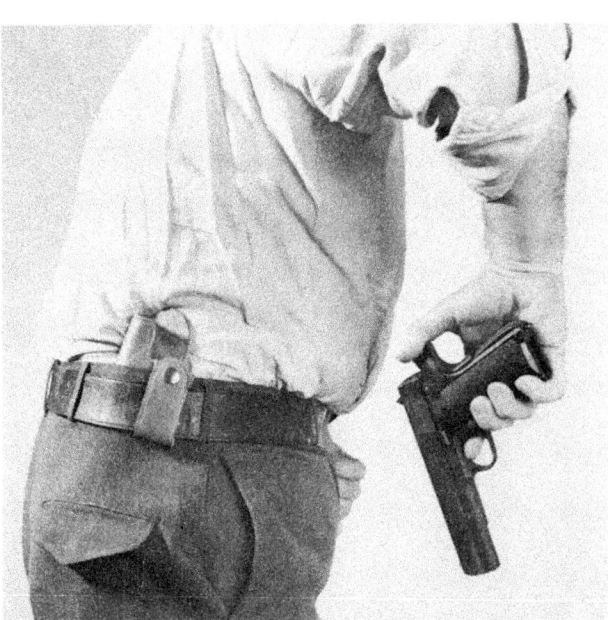 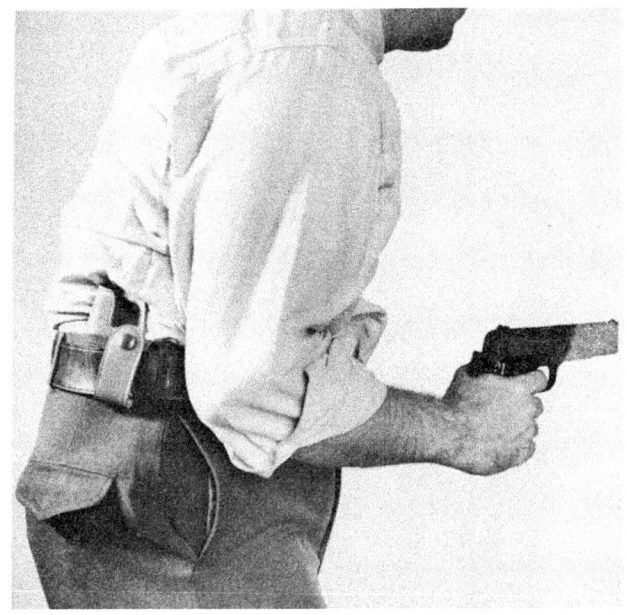

 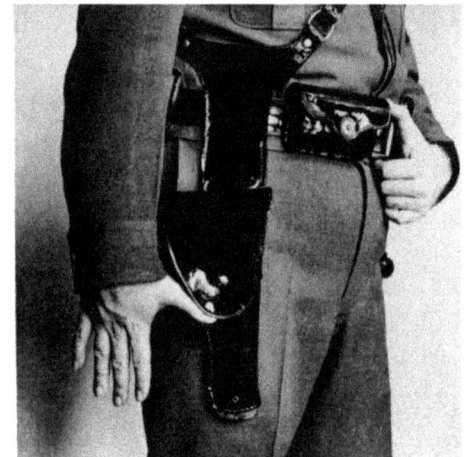 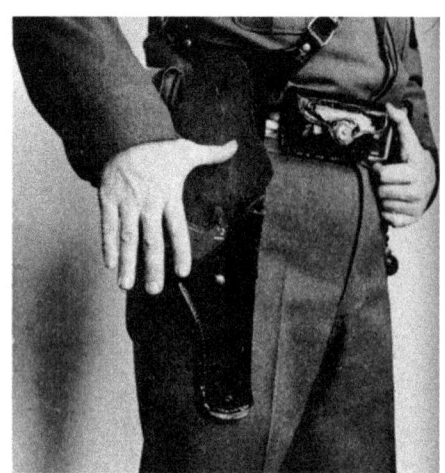

(Top row, from left to right)

(1) He lifts the flap with his extended thumb.
(2) He grasps the butt of the gun.
(3) He pulls gun about half way out of the holster — gives the butt of the pistol about a one-quarter turn away from his body so that the rear sight engages the side of the holster.
(4) Pressing the gun against his leg, he pushes sharply downward — thus pulling the slide back.
(5) He then releases the pressure on the slide as he begins to draw the gun — allowing the slide to load a round into the chamber.

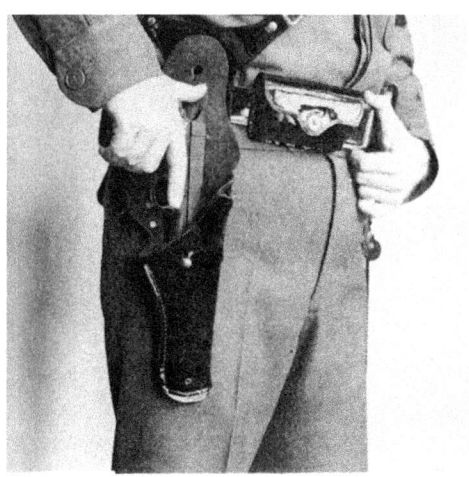

SERGEANT THOMAS B. LOUGHNAN'S DRAW

Staff Sergeant Thomas B. Loughnan, U.S.A.F., assigned to the Armed Forces Police, New York City, is the fastest man in the world today with the Government model .45 ACP and GI holster. He can grab his gun, jack a shell into the chamber, and fire an accurately placed shot faster than most men can draw and fire a double-action revolver. His time for accomplishing this feat is around a quarter of a second.

Sergeant Loughnan was gun shy at the beginning of his career and did not begin to develop his phenomenal speed and accuracy until after he was wounded. He practices a minimum of a half hour a day and is meticulous in the care and maintenance of his weapon. His weapon is an issue .45 ACP which has been altered in no way. His holster is the regulation job with only the leather block removed.

Competitive Fast Draw from Double-Action Exhibition Rigs

"Fast" is a very relative word. A police officer drawing and firing a killing shot in one-half second from his service revolver is an extremely fast man. An FBI man drawing and firing his weapon in a quarter of a second is faster still. Sergeant Loughnan drawing his .45 in the same is phenomenal. A man wearing an exhibition rig and using a double-action revolver who breaks a quarter of a second is only average. Every one hundredth of a second you whittle off the quarter of a second mark is like running a foot race up the side of a mountain — the farther you go the harder it gets.

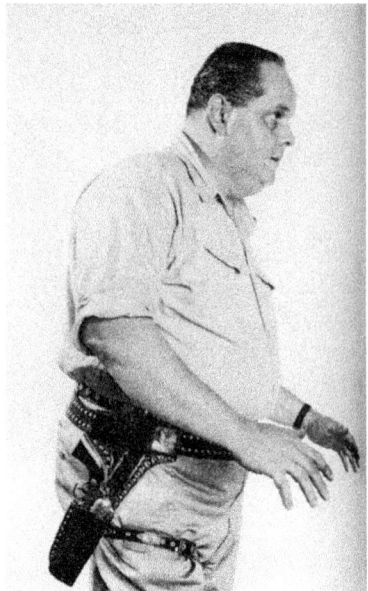

FAN LOADING THE .45 AUTOMATIC

This is an exceptionally fast method of drawing, loading, and firing the Government Model .45 Automatic.

(1) Sgt. Loughnan begins his draw as in his previous draw by opening the flap with his extended thumb.
(2) He grasps the butt of his weapon and, pressing the barrel slightly against his leg, draws gun out and forward of his holster.
(3) His gloved left hand slices backward along the slide — engaging the rear sight backward with the fanning motion.
(4) This cocks the hammer and as the slide slams forward and loads a round into the chamber,
(5) the gun is brought to bear on the target and fired.

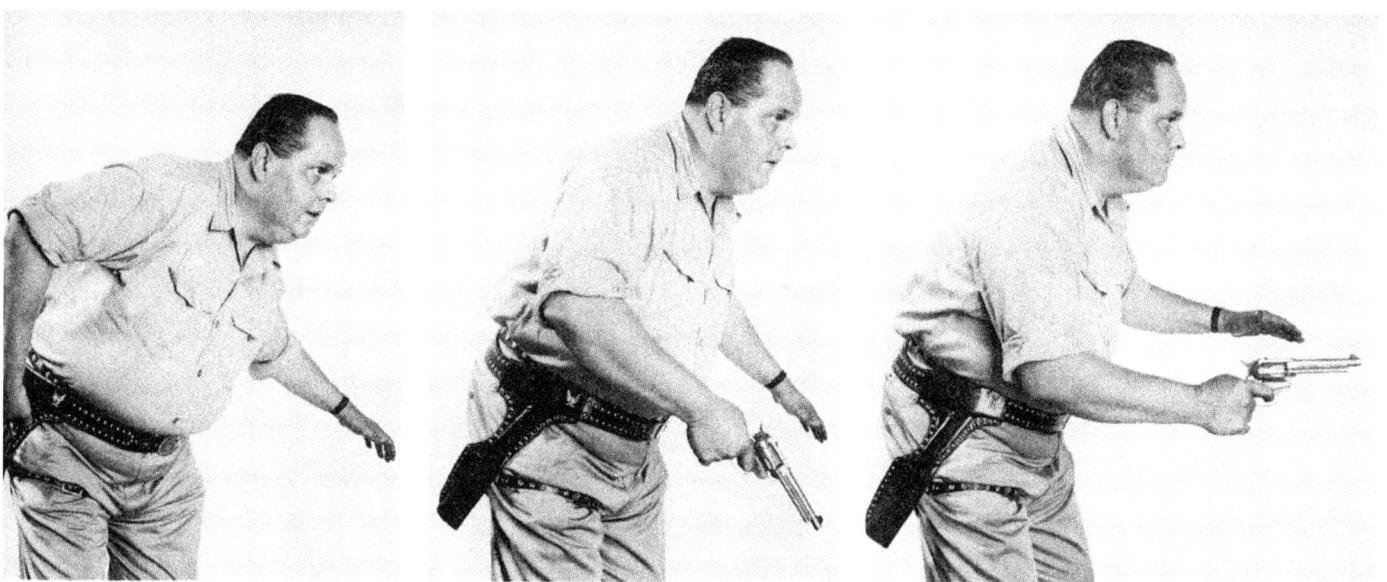

The gun is grasped and the trigger pull is begun as the weapon is pulled backward and upward into firing position.

Sizable fractions of seconds can be clipped from your drawing time by coordinating the motions of your body with those of your hand. If body motion can be used to carry the holster away from the gun as the gun is being drawn, it is obvious that a much faster draw will result.

The hand should move in one fluid, uninterrupted motion, starting as you reach for the gun and ending with the gun firing. The less distance the gun has to travel from the holster into firing position the faster your draw will be.

EXHIBITION RIGHT HIP DRAW

In this draw the hand sweeps down, picking up the butt of the gun. As the gun is thrown forward, a slight crouch will impart a backward motion to the holster. As the gun is thrown forward and upward the trigger is squeezed so that as the gun is out in firing position, the weapon fires.

This is the special steel-reinforced Gun Hawk holster designed for use with the Hi-Standard Double Nine.

EXHIBITION QUICK DRAW WITH THE GUN HAWK HOLSTER

This is the fastest possible method of drawing and firing a short-barreled revolver. The speed with which a gun can be drawn and fired in this fashion is governed almost entirely by the lock time of the gun. The gun I used in this record-breaking draw is a High-Standard Sentinel Snubnosed .22-caliber revolver with its very well-designed double-action hammer. After working over the action of this gun, the lock time is only two thirds that of the normal revolver. In this draw the gun travels only a distance of about six inches from holster to the firing position. It is small wonder that consistent draws of five and six hundredths of a second have been recorded with this gun and rig.

Close up of Gun Hawk holster and Special snubnosed Sentinel used in record draw.

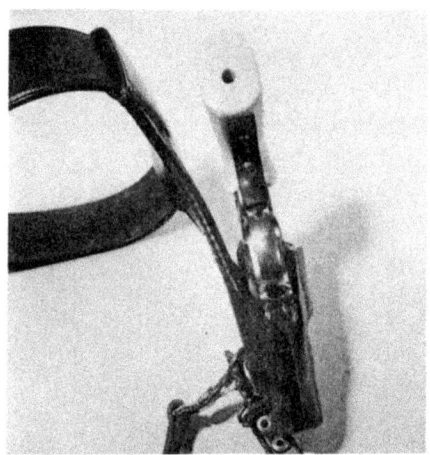 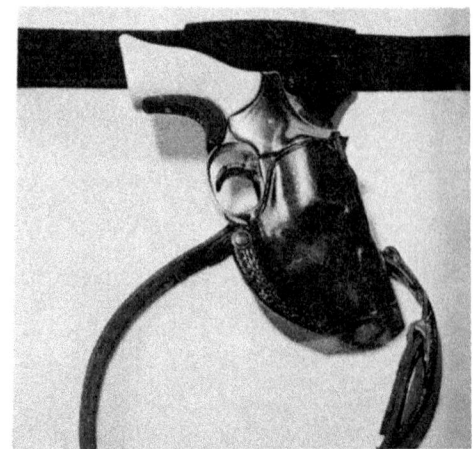

Single-Action Draw

A single-action draw consists of drawing the "knuckle-duster" — cocking it and firing. The total time of your draw depends on how rapidly you can accomplish these three tasks. If you can draw and fire a single-action gun in one third of a second in practice, you should be able to draw and fire in one quarter of a second under the stimulus of a contest. If you can do that, you can consider yourself a top gun.

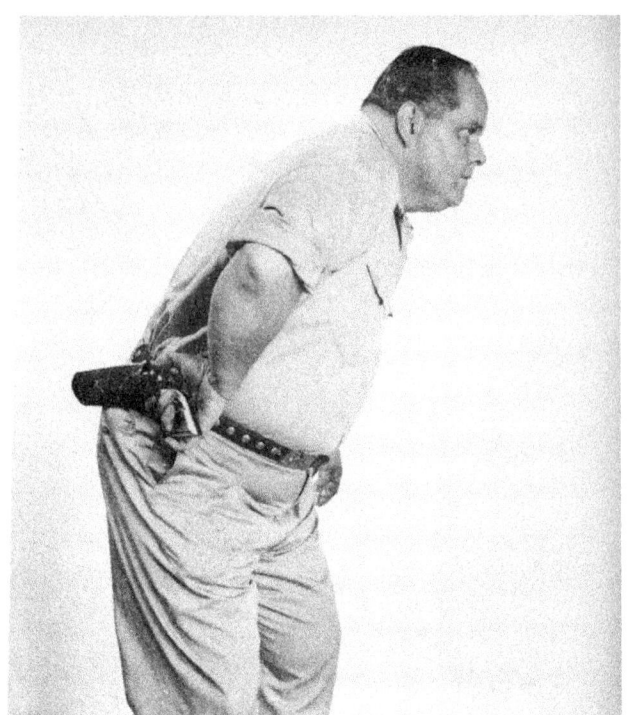

HIGH CAVALRY DRAW. This is the draw from the traditional holster. It is the only belt-type holster from which a single-action fast draw can be made while seated at a poker table, which undoubtedly accounted for its use by gamblers and gun fighters.

LOW CAVALRY DRAW with the Gun Hawk Cavalry-draw holster, demonstrated by Jess Dodge.

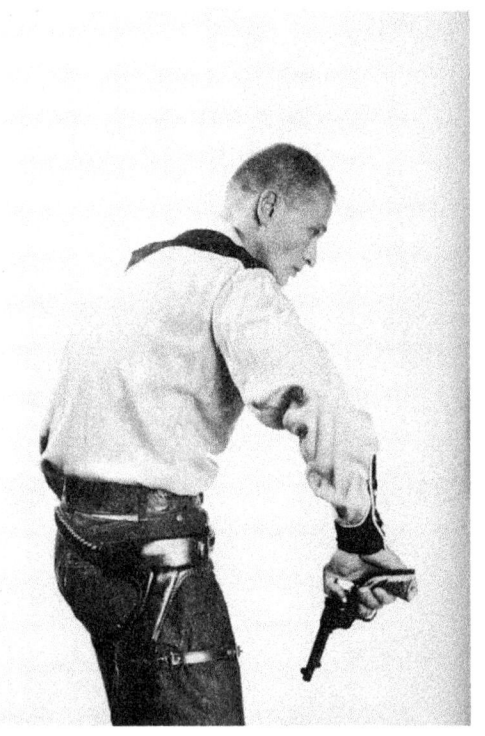

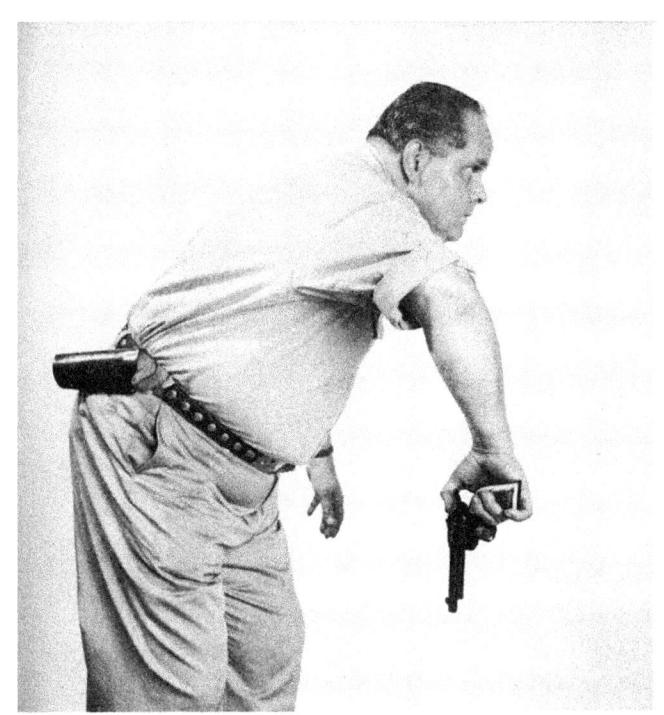

CAVALRY DRAW

The cavalry draw as used by John Wesley Hardin, Wild Bill Hickok, and Doc Holliday, is the fastest known method of drawing and firing a single-action. It is the rarest of draws today because so few will take the time to master it. It takes longer to show results than with the more conventional tied-down holster draw. This draw requires a scabbard held high with an extreme forward tilt. The revolver is held with the butt reversed and is worn just behind the right hip. The draw is begun by raising the elbow almost to shoulder height, then slamming the hand back onto the

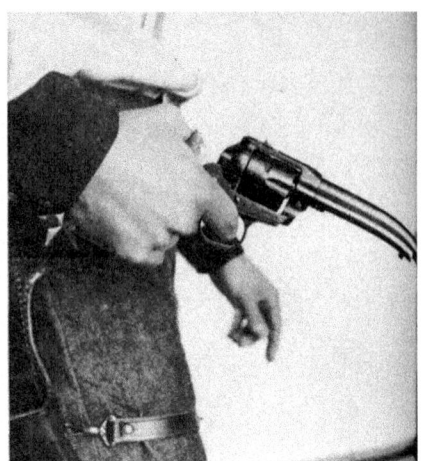

Single-action draw from the Gun Hawk holster.

reversed gun butt with the thumb across the hammer. The gun is then thrown forward out of the holster as the elbow is snapped down to the side. This whips the gun around into firing position. The weight of the gun against the thumb cocks the gun with no conscious effort on the shooter's part. All that's left for you to do is fire. The gun should be fired the instant it is on target.

Cavalry draw can be even faster if slip shooting is used. A slip gun is one with the trigger removed or tied back and the hammer spur ground smooth, lower, and shorter. With this draw the hammer is grasped with the webbing between thumb and forefinger. As the gun is snapped forward and comes into firing position, you tighten your grip on the butt of the gun and the hammer slips free, firing the weapon.

Slip-shooting is not so accurate as firing the gun in the normal way, but there is nothing faster. I must caution you gunslicks once again to use only blank cartridges or wax bullets.

TIED DOWN

An extremely fast draw from a low-slung right-hand-draw holster can be made only if the holster is rigid. Holster and belt slippage add too much time to your draw. The holster should be canted backward and should be so rigid that when your hand hits the gun, only the gun moves. Holsters worn with the gun at fingertip level are not so fast as ones with the gun butt riding at wrist or forearm height. An arm fully extended and hanging straight cannot move with the speed and acceleration of an arm slightly bent.

Do exercises to strengthen your grip, wrist, and forearm and you will find noticeable increase in your speed of draw. I have known of men who practiced with solid lead castings on their guns, so that when they used their real shooting irons it was child's play.

 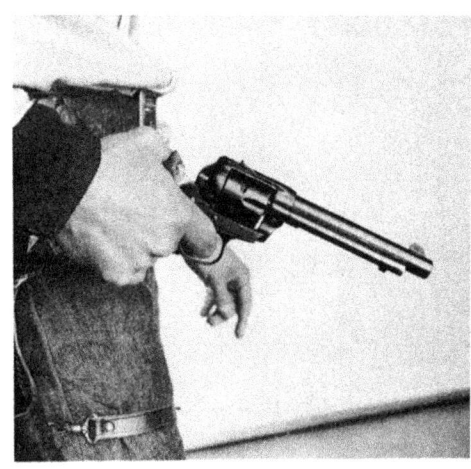

(Left) Wrong method of cocking single-action.

(Right) Correct method — gives a positive control of hammer action.

Don't go in for a lot of gun twirling if you have any respect for your gun and holster. Curley Bill Brocius was the only gunfighter on the frontier who went in for such nonsense, and it's said that he was downed while his gun was still whirling in the air. In my misspent youth, I must confess, I went in for a bit of plain and fancy juggling, but it didn't improve my shooting a bit. I perfected a beautiful, flashy, one-finger draw that twirled the gun up out of the holster, cocked and in firing position. It impressed no end of tyros even greener than myself, and it was a wonderful thing to behold as it soared up out of the holster spinning like a silver dervish in the sunlight. As a sort of Fourth-of-July display of pyrotechnics it was ginger-peachy — but it could have gotten me killed in a gun fight. It took almost two full seconds from draw to shot.

To attain a really fast draw, it is necessary to eliminate all waste motions and shorten the distance traveled from the holster to the firing position. You should practice your draw in front of a mirror. This way, you can correct many of your own mistakes.

One of the most common points of error, of the single-action draw from a side holster, is the manner in which the thumb contacts the hammer spur. The wrong way, which a majority of fast-draw shooters use, is to place the ball of the thumb along the hammer spur with the thumb parallel to the length of the hammer. This method of cocking the gun adds about one tenth of a second to your draw time. The thumb should slam in crosswise on the hammer spur between the first and second joint. The thumb rides in the curved depression toward the forward part of the hammer. This is a much more positive method of cocking the gun. It is both safer and faster. When grabbing the gun in this fashion, you are able to get a much better grip on the butt. The hammer is cocked back as the gun is drawn backward and upward out of the holster into firing position. The gun is fully cocked as it nears the firing position and thus can be fired the instant it is in line with the target.

Quick Draw 141

Fanning with the Ringo holster.

Time can be shaved from a fast draw by bending the knees and dropping into a crouch as the gun is being whipped from the holster. The motion of the legs drops the holster an inch or so away from the gun, reducing the time necessary to clear the holster.

CROSS DRAW—RINGO HOLSTER

The cross draw with a single-action can be very fast, as the Ringo Kid, Johnny Ringo, proved on the frontier. The holster should be a high scabbard firmly attached to a snug belt and worn forward of the left hip. The shooter should stand with the target in line with the point only slightly forward of his left shoulder. He then twists his waist from left to right, bringing the holstered gun to meet his reaching hand halfway. As the shooter grasps the butt of the gun and begins to pull it from the holster, he twists his middle back from right to left, whipping the holster away from the gun. As the shooter locks his arm and gun hand tightly against his body, he brings his gloved left hand swiftly back across the hammer, fanning it into a fully-cocked position. The gun is then fired across the body.

Under almost all conditions, fanning is so inaccurate that it is not worth while contemplating. You can get a fair degree of accuracy while fanning if you take a lot of time — but that defeats its own purpose. In this draw, with the arm braced against your body, if you use fanning only for cocking you get pretty fair accuracy.

Drop The Dollar

I have never seen a shooter who didn't secretly believe that he was very fast in handling a gun. To accuse a man of being slow on the draw is almost like questioning the virtue of a member of the opposite sex. Very few people are even reasonably competent judges of their own speed, let alone that of someone else. If we were able to compute one hundredths of a second accurately there wouldn't be any market for stop watches. Other than electronic timers, which are quite expensive and are nowhere near as infallibly accurate as we would like them to be, there are much easier and simpler ways of checking your progress in gunslickery.

For the beginner, all that is needed is one battered old felt hat with as wide a brim as possible. For this trick in self-timing you hold the hat out in the right hand, rim downward, at about shoulder height. You drop the hat, sweep your hand down, draw your gun, and try to catch the parachuting hat on the end of your gun barrel. Don't be surprised if you can't do it the first few times, because although it seems to fall very slowly, it actually takes slightly less than a second before it hits the ground. When you can whip your gun out and catch the hat at waist height, you are drawing at less than a half second. This shows you are well on the way to becoming as fast as you thought you were.

Next take a nice shiny dollar — or if you don't feel like throwing your money around, a one-and-a-half-inch steel washer will do. Hold the coin on the back of your hand with your arm extending at shoulder level. Sweep your arm downward from under the weight, draw your weapon, and try to click the hammer before it hits the ground. Again, don't be disappointed if

DROP THE HAT

DROP THE DOLLAR

you can't do it. The time you are running against is roughly two fifths of a second. With some constant practice in front of a mirror you will soon be beating it — not much, but a little. Next, lower your hand to waist height with the "iron man" or washer on the back of your hand. You are now being timed at approximately one quarter of a second. I have a friend, a New York City policeman, who can drop a dime from shoulder height, shoot, and hit it at waist height with his service gun from a special double-action rig. Many a hoodlum has given up the idea of shooting it out with this officer after seeing his split-second draw.

If you're sure you are getting your draw down below a fifth of a second, go to the hardware store and buy one of those little light blinker buttons. Get hold of an old floor lamp and plug it in. Put the blinker button in the socket and screw in a forty-watt light bulb. Draw your gun as the light goes on and see if you can fire before it goes out and comes on again. This will give you good practice in recognizing a signal, drawing, and firing. The blinker lights are usually set for about one tenth of a second for each phase.

Quick-draw clubs have sprung up all over the country. Many fast-draw contests are being held. When you enter these contests, do so for the fun of it. When you go up against someone who is faster, and you undoubtedly will, don't let it get you down, watch him closely and see what you can learn about his technique that can help you. Maybe the next time around you'll be the top gun.

CHAPTER 21

The Psychology of Gun Fighting

THE PEACE OFFICER who is psychologically unprepared for a gunfight is fighting two men when he goes into combat. He must conquer both himself and his adversary. Every year many policemen are wounded or killed because they hesitated to shoot or tried to give some gunman a "break." A classic example of this was a very good friend of mine in the Pennsylvania State Police. A juvenile psycho was holding two other troopers at bay with a double-barreled shotgun, when my friend came up from the rear. He drew his gun and started to shoot the crazed youth in the back. He must have felt that he couldn't shoot the lad, who was unaware of his presence. He decided to sneak up and disarm him. The youth heard his approach, whirled, and nearly decapitated him with blasts from both barrels of his gun. If the trooper hadn't been such a nice guy, he'd be alive today. One well-placed shot from his service revolver would have prevented the tragedy.

Most of a police officer's training is devoted to protecting and saving life. It takes a definite adjustment on his part to know when to take a life. In most cases, police officers have been shot because they hesitated to shoot first. The armed hoodlum, in the majority of cases, has already made his decision to kill rather than to be apprehended. Frequently a felon will draw his gun and shoot even after the police officer has confronted him with a drawn gun. When apprehending a thug at gun point, an officer should have his mind made up to shoot at the first indication of resistance.

The law-enforcement officer should also school himself to shoot instantly and accurately when he draws his gun in a gun fight. Then it is foolish for a policeman to shoot to wound, rather than kill, an armed man he is endeavoring to apprehend. Very few men are such superb marksmen that they can call their shots in the heat of battle. The officer who tries to overpower or disarm a thug is not only an optimist, he is a fool. Any felon who decides to shoot it out with the law should be shot.

One of the most expert and efficient gun fighters I have come across survived his first combat only because his adversary ran out of ammunition. He told me that during the battle he was confronted with the appalling knowledge that he didn't know what to do in a gun fight. Fortunately for him, the gunman he was trying to arrest was as miserable a marksman as he himself. After he was rescued by the patrolman in the sector car, he swore to himself that this would never happen to him again. To this very day, he says, he has occasional nightmares in which he can almost smell the burned cordite in that dim Harlem tenement hallway.

His first move was to seek expert advice. He adapted his service weapon to give him the "edge" in any future conflict. He bought hand-loading equipment and "rolled his own" practice loads and custom service ammunition. He studied the most effective combat techniques, and he still shoots up around a thousand rounds a week. He has decided that in any situation that calls for a gun fight he will shoot first and shoot to kill. Since that first frustrating fiasco he has been in half-a-dozen gun fights in which he was the decisive victor. In the last two such shootouts, he won against three-to-one odds, which he now feels, as the result of his training, are just about even.

One of the most common human traits is to refuse to believe the imminence of one's own death or painful injury. In Nazi Germany thousands of people marched docilely to what the experience of others should have taught them was certain death. These people simply refused to believe that such a catastrophe was happening to them. Despite some opinions to the contrary, policemen are human beings and they are prey to many of the same unrealistic attitudes as their civilian brothers. In fact, they are more vulnerable in this sense than are most civilians: because of the authority with which society has endowed them, they refuse to believe that any felon would really try to kill them. If the thug is not a poor marksman, it's too late for them to change their evaluation of the situation.

Unless a man has made up his mind what he will do in combat, he may fall easy prey to panic. A recent survey, conducted in a large metropolitan police force, showed that in the majority of cases where police officers were engaged in gun duels, they were shooting wildly, firing their revolvers double-action even at distances of more than one hundred yards. Yet many of those same policemen had expert ratings on the target range. It is not unusual to read of running gunfights during which more than fifty rounds were fired, all of them misses! One well-aimed shot could have wound things up in the beginning.

The best way to avoid danger and often fatal panic in a gun fight is to condition both your mind and your reflexes to react to danger in a manner that will give you a fighting chance when the chips are down. This can be accomplished only through repeated mental and physical exercise. You must establish in your mind an acceptance of the idea that *you may be forced to take a human life*. You must condition your reflexes to such a degree that drawing, aiming, and firing a gun are almost automatic reactions to mortal danger. Constant practice of these physical and mental exercises may not guarantee you infallibly against panic in a shootout, but it is unquestionably the best solution to the problem. No person can ever be absolutely certain how he will react to any given set of circumstances, but any measure of preparedness is always preferable to unpreparedness.

Unfortunately, the realization of the need for preparedness is always the aftermath of a shocking experience. One police officer, whom I have known for some time, underwent conditioning of this type after his brother, also a police officer, was seriously wounded in a gun fight. Less than a year after this his training was of immeasurable help in a gun fight with a felon who had killed several officers in making previous escapes from arrest. But, cases such as his are the exception and not the rule. Federal and state law-enforcement agencies stress these psychological factors in their training programs. One result of this training is that you never read of cases of ineffective action on their part in the daily press. The refusal of municipal governments to face reality in this matter has been responsible for the sacrifice of a great many lives, both of police and of innocent bystanders.

Perhaps this can all be summed up best by the advice an old-time peace officer gave to me many years ago, "If you can't shoot faster than the other fellow, make damn good and sure you shoot straighter."

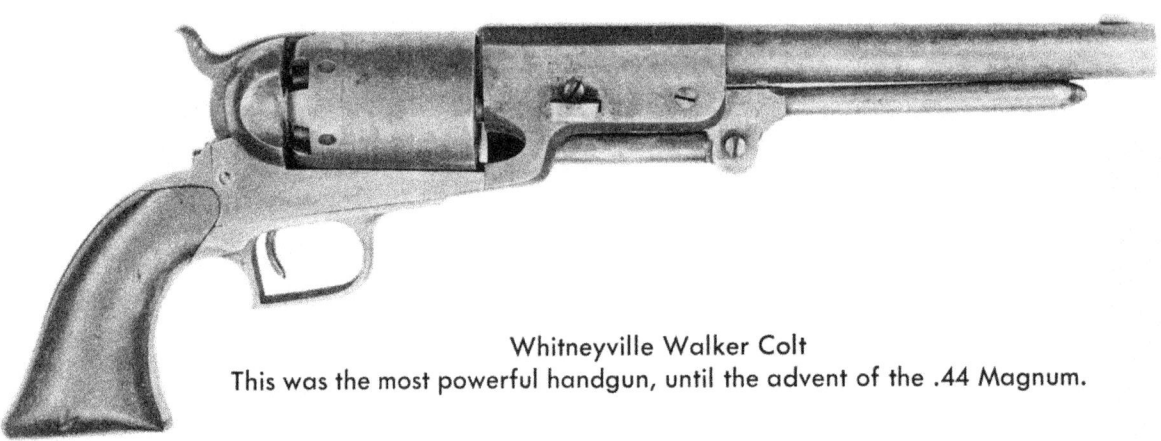
Whitneyville Walker Colt
This was the most powerful handgun, until the advent of the .44 Magnum.

CHAPTER 22

Holster History

IN THE LATE seventeenth and early eighteenth centuries handguns fell into three general classifications. First, there was the large and quite effective "horse pistol," the best answer to the "Stand and deliver!" of the highwayman. It was carried by mounted men, either strapped to the saddle or tucked in a saddlebag. Very large and heavy, this gun was much too cumbersome to carry on the person.

The second type was the "belt pistol," which, stuck beneath the belt or sash, was carried in hunting or in war as a last-ditch weapon. These guns, lighter and less cumbersome than the horse pistols, as a rule were not so effective.

The third type consisted of the small and quite ineffective "pocket pistols." These ranged from the rather respectable-sized heavy-bore pistols carried in greatcoat pockets to the very small pistols worn in the vest pockets of eighteenth-century fops and dandies, to scare off the cutpurses and thieves who infested the cities.

Most of these eighteenth-century pistols were single-shot weapons and were never holstered. The first appearance of anything resembling holsters was the wide leather crossbelt, worn bandolier fashion on one shoulder by artillerymen. On this belt were sewn from six to eight small holsters, each holding an all-metal single-shot pistol. Quickly adopted by naval gunners, it also found instant favor with pirates and privateers because of the superior firepower it afforded.

Equipment used in making Missouri Skintite on early frontier (above)

Opposite page (left to right):
- Wet leather is folded for belt loop
- Wet leather is molded around gun
- Leather is nailed to board around outline of gun
- Holster is allowed to dry in sun and shrink around gun
- Excess leather is trimmed
- Finished holster is shown with rawhide lacing through the nail holes

By the late eighteenth century saddle holsters slung over the pommel became common with both cavalry units and travelers. With the advent of single-action cap-and-ball pistols, the big saddle holsters were a necessity. But it was not until Sam Colt invented the cap-and-ball revolver that holsters really began to come into their own. Some cavalry officers were known to have as many as four Paterson Colt revolvers in saddle holsters, slung in pairs forward of and behind the saddle. Frequently they would have one or more pistols tucked in their belts. This was not too comfortable for a man on horseback, besides being an unsafe way to carry these valuable sidearms, so many of the officers began adapting the saddle holsters for belt use.

Some of the Colt Dragoon pistols were carried in belt holsters, but they were intended primarily as horse pistols. The smaller Colt pocket pistols often were carried in holsters, but the belt holster didn't reach full bloom of popularity until about the time of the Civil War. The Navy Colt was the

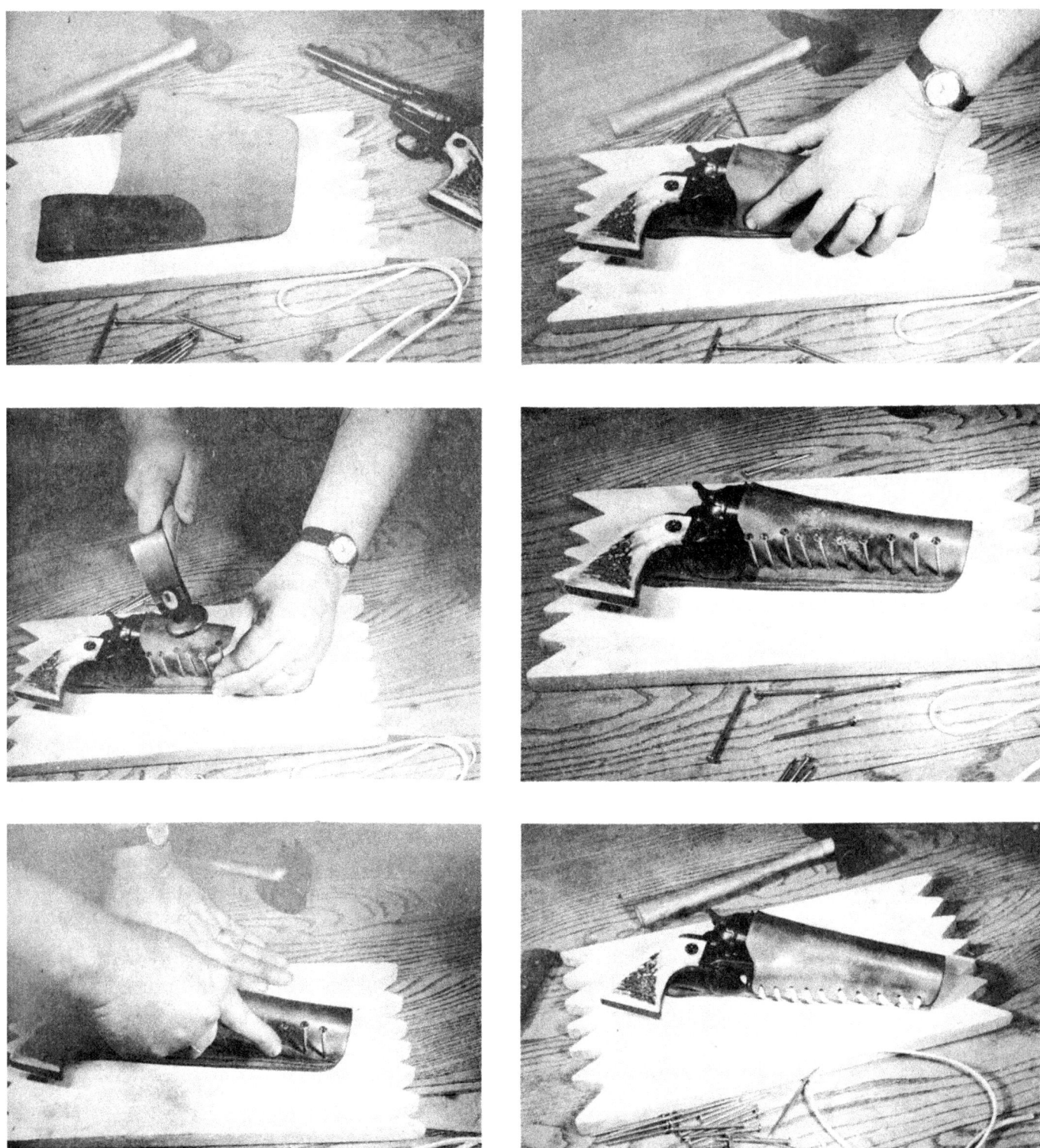

first gun generally carried in a belt holster. The cavalry holster was a left-handed stiff-leather job, with a flap held in place by a brass stud. It completely enveloped the Navy Colt and was not unlike the GI holster of today. Its sole virtue was that it protected the gun. The holster was left-handed because a cavalryman was trained to wield his saber in his right hand and use the newfangled pistol in his left hand, for emergencies only.

However, in combat the trooper soon preferred to use the six-shot Colt as his primary weapon and save the saber as his last-ditch defense. War Department files contain many communiqués from commanding officers of cavalry units, stating that the Colt revolver had made the saber an obsolete weapon. The use of this left-handed holster by a right-handed man resulted in the cavalry draw, which is to this day the fastest method of drawing and firing a single-action revolver.

The bushwhackers and the jayhawkers along the Kansas and Missouri border took the Civil War personally. They changed the existing holsters to fit the guerrilla warfare that raged in that area. They started by cutting off the flap of the cavalry holster and then used an "Arkansas toothpick" to whittle away a liberal amount of leather as unnecessary. This made their handguns instantly accessible and constituted the birth of fast-draw gun fighting.

Their cut-down holsters soon became ripped and torn as made-over holsters always do, and so the border bushwhackers developed their own method of holster making. They soaked a piece of heavy cowhide in water, then, folding the wet leather around their gun, trimmed off the excess leather. The reverse side of the hide was rubbed with the shinbone of a lamb, smoothing the fibers of the leather. Then they nailed the leather tightly around the gun to a flat board, putting the nails no more than half an inch apart. The gun and the half-made holster were then put out in the broiling sun; the wet leather quickly dried and shrank around the gun. They trimmed the leather about a quarter inch to the outside of the nails. When the nails were removed from the board, a rawhide thong was laced through the nail holes. This type of holster was called the Missouri Skintite and when made with reasonable care and skill was a better-fitting job than are most holsters sold today.

Later, many of the professional gun fighters cut the top of the holster down still farther, usually to a point midway in the cylinder of the revolver. The belt loop was lowered to raise the butt of the gun above the belt on which it was carried. These rigs were called the Outlaw or Half-breed Holster, and when a man went into town wearing one he was given a wide berth.

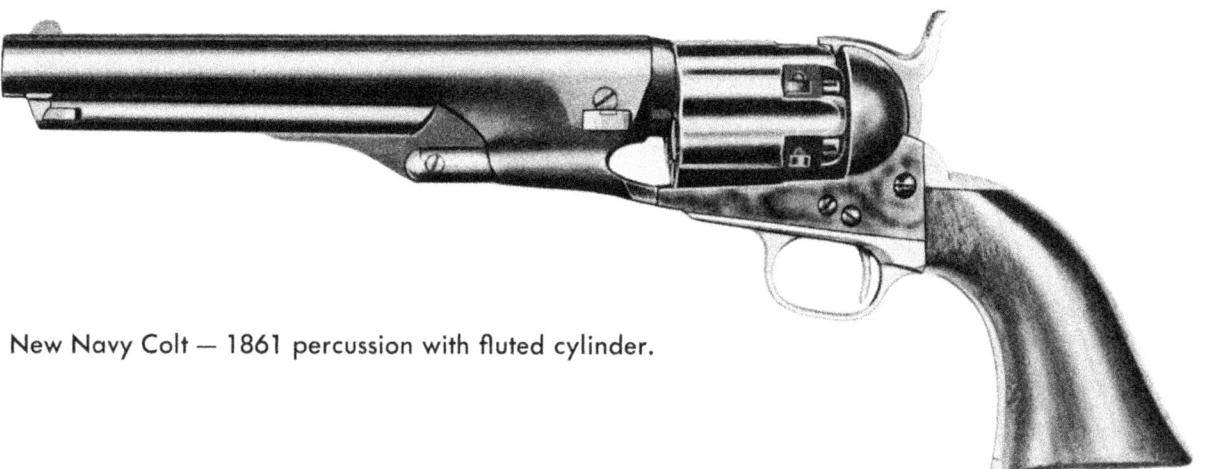

New Navy Colt — 1861 percussion with fluted cylinder.

The cavalry-draw Skintite and the Outlaw Holster, with countless modifications as to angle, remained the favorites of the gun fighters throughout the badman era. This included the few gun fighters who preferred cross draw — for the cross-draw scabbard was only a left-handed man's cavalry-draw Skintite, used by a right-handed man for cross draw.

The exact origin of the shoulder holster is not known. However, various gun fighters were quite ingenious in designing their own variations. There were some "shoulder scabbards" in use during the Civil War, but these were little more than the conventional belt scabbard attached to a rather crude shoulder harness — Jesse James was reputed to have concealed his guns in this fashion at times. Some people credit Ben Thompson with the invention of the shoulder holster, but it was actually in use before his time. Legend has it that the spring-clip shoulder holster first saw the light of day in a Colorado mining town — Central City, Leadville, and Cripple Creek all have claimed that honor. Luke Short and Doc Holliday both used the shoulder rig for their second or holdout guns. Short is supposed to have had his made in St. Louis, for one of the first Colt .45-caliber double-action "Lightning" revolvers to show up on the frontier. Doc Holliday brought his back from a trip to Denver, so the story goes. The shoulder holster soon became a favorite with the hordes of Pinkerton detectives hired by the railroads and cattlemen's associations. Many gamblers favored the spring-clip shoulder rig almost as much as they did the wrist holster for the Derringer. However, because of its small size and the shape of its butt, the Derringer could be rocked out of a vest pocket or trousers watch pocket with a speed far greater than any holster could offer.

In the waning years of the nineteenth century, when the badman and the gun fighter were already legend-shrouded, a change began to come

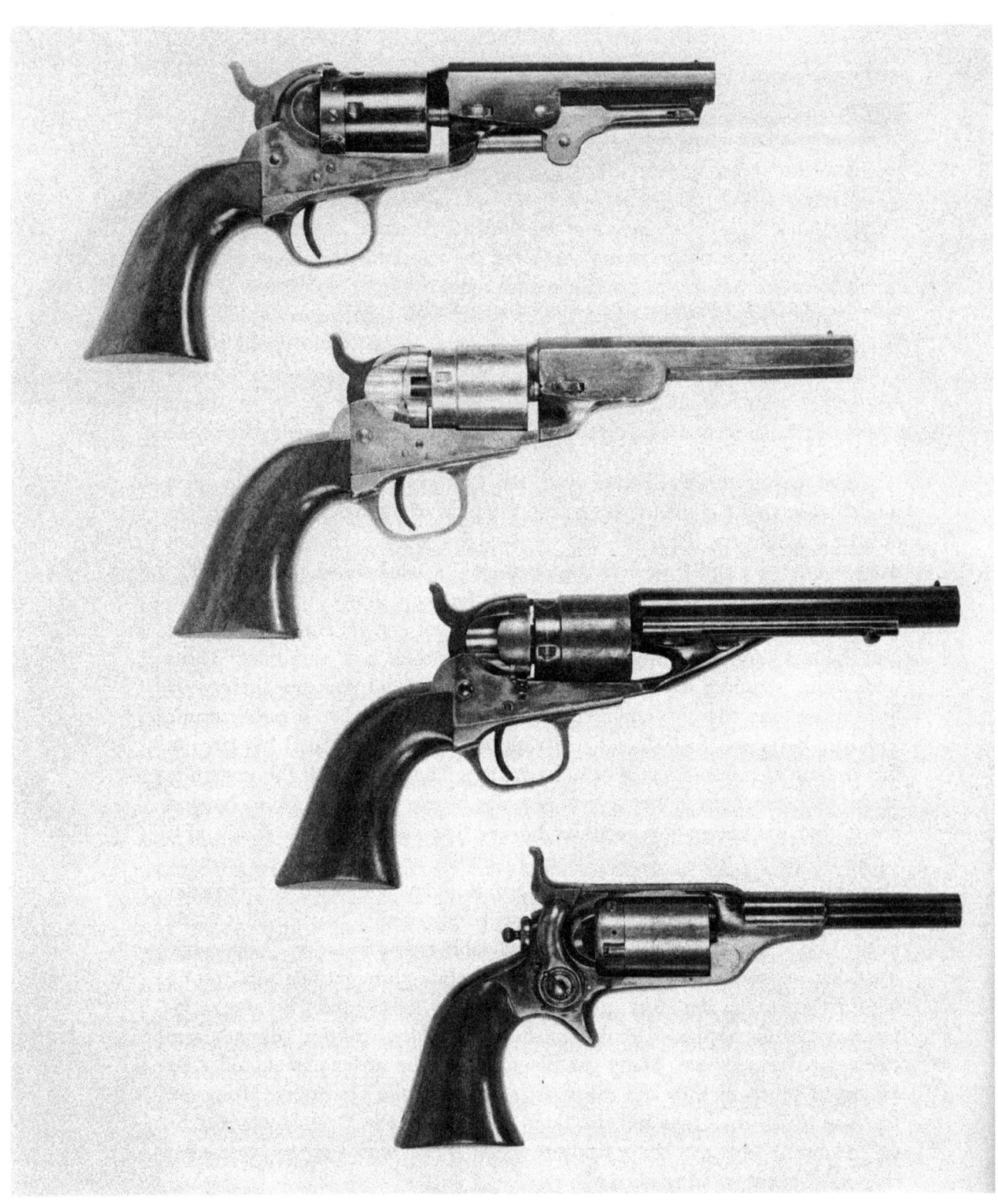

Thuer Conversion of Pocket Pistol of 1849
.38 R M Conversion of the Navy Pocket Pistol
.38 R M Conversion of Pocket Pistol
1855 Root Side Hammer Metallic Conversion

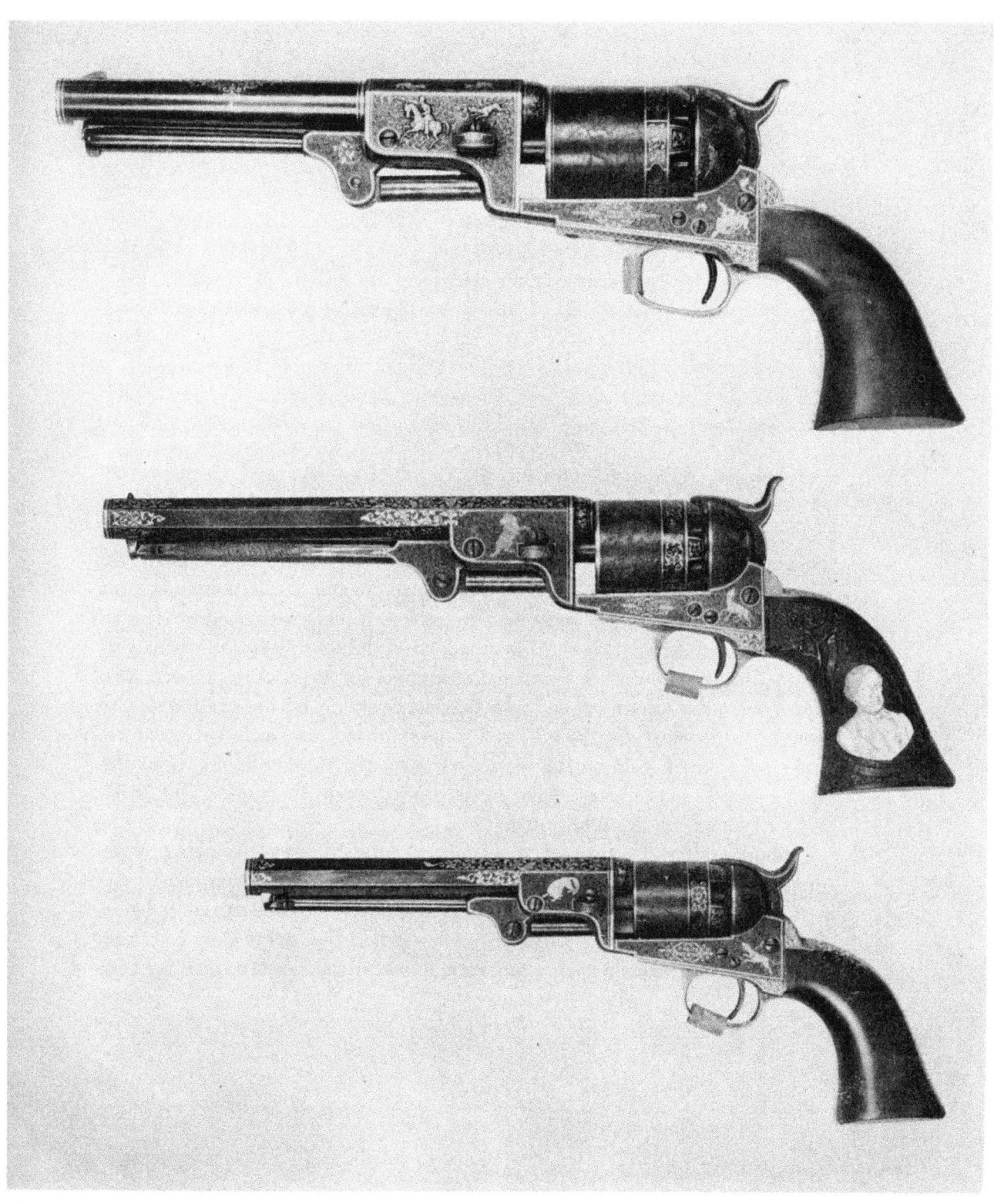

Three Engraved Colt Presentation Revolvers
3rd Model Dragoon
Old Navy Colt — 1851
Old Pocket Colt — 1849

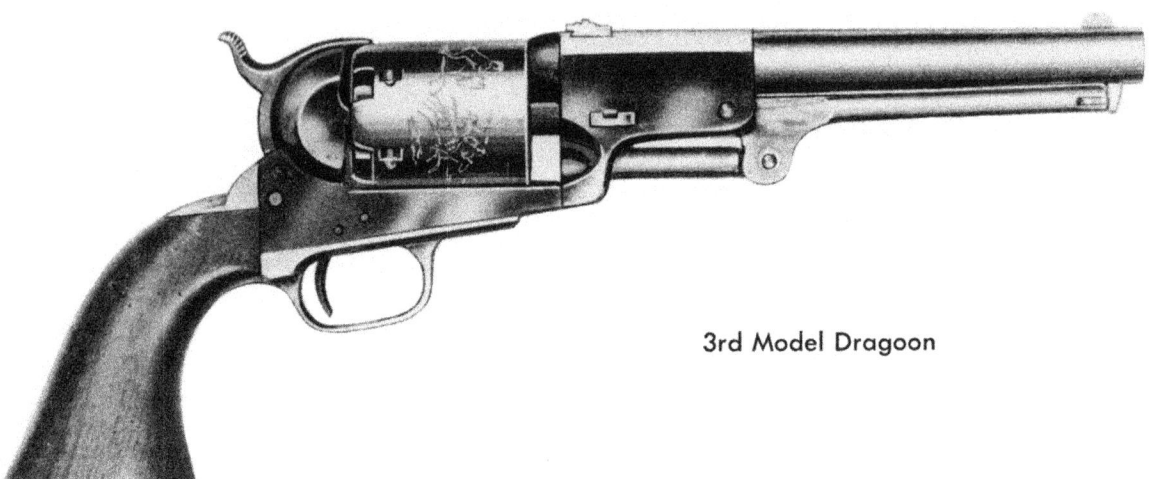

3rd Model Dragoon

over holsters. It was not one for the better. Cowboys and sheepherders whiled away the long winter nights in the bunkhouse by fashioning holsters and gunbelts for themselves, each man trying to make his rig fancier than the next one's. The clean, functional lines of the Skintite and Outlaw rig were soon lost in a maze of heavy leg flaps, straps, studs, conchos, and buckles. The gun became more and more lost in an overpowering display of ornamented leather. Much of it was done in dubious imitation of the rigs dreamed up by New York theatrical costumers for Wild West shows. Also copied were the ornate fringed and beaded buckskin holsters fashioned by reservation Indians for long-haired buckskin-clad mustachioed mountebanks, who struck gold on the lecture circuits and vaudeville shows of the mauve decade. As holsters, these monstrosities might be termed the "Redskin's Revenge" on the white man.

Shortly after the turn of the century, tourists began bringing wide, ornately carved and silver-mounted gun belts north from Mexico. In the slots of these belts were suspended either one or two equally ornate holsters. These ponderous bits of impedimenta were called *buscadero* rigs. Anything so eye catching, bearing such a romantic name, was a surefire sales item for

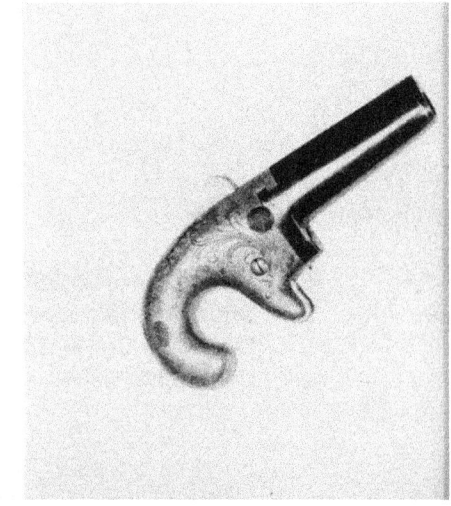

Colt and National Derringers *(Left to right)*
Colt #1 National Derringer .41 Cal.
Colt #2 National Derringer .41 Rim Fire
Colt #3 Thuer Derringer First Type .41 Rim Fire
Colt #4 Thuer Derringer Second Type .41 Rim Fire

the "gringo touristas" who took them home to wear on ceremonial occasions. Mexican *vaqueros* continued to carry their guns in well-designed, well-made, fast-draw rigs, while the *buscadero* hung on as tourist bait. Some were later made in this country. Saddlemakers, with little or no knowledge of gun fighting, continued to manufacture these ersatz antiques. It was inevitable that anything so exotic and so totally lacking in authenticity would catch the eye of Hollywood producers who were discovering the West. And what Hollywood found, television rediscovered when the cathode tube took over.

Around the turn of the century, the gun-fighting peace officers were desperately seeking ways to make their draw faster than that of the outlaws in the Arizona territory and in the pockets of lawlessness that were spread wide throughout the West.

This was the period of the gimmick holster. Studs were welded onto the sides of guns. They fitted into metal-rimmed slots in the gun belt. The guns could then be swiveled or slid out of the slot for a fast draw. These were an offshoot of the open-end holsters suspended from the belt on swivels. With this type of holster, the gun was swiveled up into a horizontal position and fired through the holster. The trouble with both of these devices was that it is next to impossible to hit anything with a handgun fired in this fashion. To overcome this inaccuracy, Ed McGivern designed a pair of cutaway holsters that snapped free of the belt.

There was one holster prevalent at that time that could easily have been designed by Rube Goldberg. As the gun was holstered, you forced it downward, compressing a heavy spring at the bottom of the scabbard. The gun was caught and retained in the holster with a catch that could be released by pressing a button on the gun belt. When you pressed this release, the gun catapulted out of the holster into (if you were lucky) your waiting hand.

Some of the foxier grandpas went in for holsters sewn into their hip

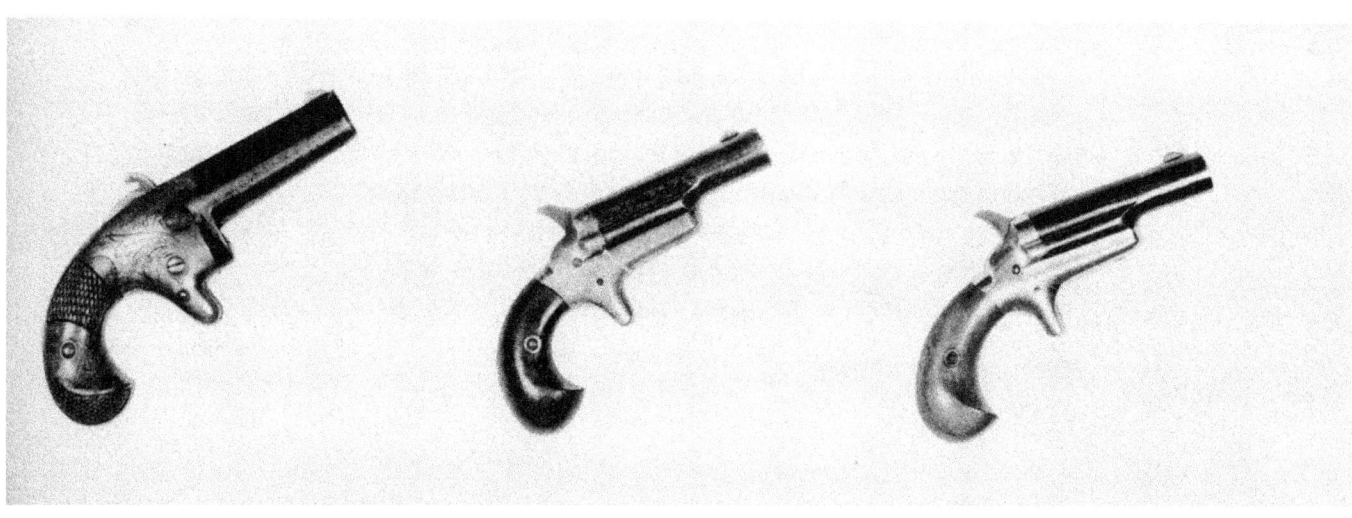

pockets. These were reasonably fast, although I can't say much for their comfort.

At that time a half-breed Indian with a distinguished record as a peace officer, Tom Threepersons, designed a fine holster. He took the old Skintite Outlaw holster, raised it higher on the belt, and canted it butt forward to a marked degree. This holster, as made by the late "Tio Sam" Myers, was perhaps the best holster of that era. With minor modifications, it is the issue holster of the FBI today.

The Threepersons holster was so fast that, to all intents and purposes, it made all the gimmick rigs obsolete. In the twentieth century very little was done to change or improve holsters. Clark of California designed a spring-clip "across-the-body" draw holster that has met with considerable favor with police officers around the country. The Berns-Martin "Lightning" upside-down shoulder holster is an original and effective design.

The Myers Border Patrol holster is one of the best service holsters designed.

Otherwise, the commercial output in the last fifty years has been in a sorry state, with each man tending to copy the mistakes of his competitors and no one conscientiously thinking of the needs of the man who must wear a gun. Not one peace officer in a hundred today carries his gun in a holster that is anything but a definite hazard.

CHAPTER 23

The Shooting Gallery

WHENEVER gun talk drifts around to tales of mortal combat, and it always does, the names of a few super "gunslicks" of the Old West always crop up. At such times voices as well as tempers rise in defense of the lethal talents of these top guns — as if they needed any defending in the first place!

I have never heard of an instance where two super-fast gunmen shot it out with each other. When two of them met, as they frequently did, their relationship was usually cordial, or anyway circumspect. Invariably during an altercation one or the other would back down. Far from casting a shadow on the character, courage, or capabilities of the man who did the backing down, it speaks well for his common sense.

With two men who had attained the ultimate speed in fast-draw combat, the likeliest outcome of such a duel would be that they would kill each other. These men fattened their purses and built their reputations by counting on the fraction of a second's edge that they held over the average man. These top guns also had equipment superior to that of the men they went up against. The files of the Colt's Patent Firearms Manufacturing Company of Hartford, Connecticut, hold correspondence from Bat Masterson ordering a pair of .45-caliber Colt Single-actions, with four-and-three-quarter inch barrels, and specifying details as to how the gunsmith should customize the actions. The top gun fighters ordered their weapons through their gunsmiths and had them add final details. They also designed their own holsters and either made them themselves or had them made by a saddlemaker.

In contrast, the average cowboy bought his .45 by mail order, or got it third or fourth hand. He frequently used it as a hammer, a crowbar, or any other tool needed at the time. He usually wore it in a holster handed down from Army use. Often as not it was made in such a fashion that it would take a search warrant to get the gun out. Too often it turned out to be his death warrant when he went up against a fast man.

These gunmen sold their guns to the highest bidders, regardless of which side of the law they were on at the time. It was not uncommon for a man to be a peace officer in one county and a wanted man in all counties surrounding his bailiwick.

Here is my own personal appraisal of some of the top gun fighters of the frontier:

WYATT EARP
during his later years in California

Wyatt Earp

Mr. Earp was the one man in the rolls of top-flight gun fighters who was not very fast on the draw. He had nerves of chilled steel and would allow his enemy to take one or two fast shots at him while he deliberately took aim and coolly shot him down. Earp's score didn't begin to tally with his brothers-at-arms. Although far from the best, he was one of the very few who lived out his "threescore and ten."

DOC HOLLIDAY
A rare picture of Holliday

Doc Holliday

In my opinion, Doc Holliday was one of the most dangerous men of his time. Because he was a dying man, he took risks that no sensible man would ever take. He was absolutely ruthless, and when Doc decided he was going to kill a man, that man was as good as dead. He was lightning fast with both handgun and knife. He carried two revolvers, one in a shoulder clip, the other in a cavalry-draw scabbard at his hip. He also carried a Bowie knife in a sheath beneath his frock coat. Doc died of tuberculosis in the hospital of a small Colorado town. When assured by nurses that his boots were off, he said, "This is ridiculous," and fell back dead.

Harvey Logan

Logan holds the dubious honor of being officially credited with more killings than any other gun fighter. He was the executioner for the Wild Bunch, also known as the Hole-in-the-Wall Gang. Butch Cassidy and the Sundance Kid may have been more famed in song and story, but they couldn't hold a candle to Harvey Logan when it came to just plain killing. For years, under the alias of Kid Curry, Logan was the most-wanted man in the West. He was known to have ridden for several days just to rub out a rancher who had informed on a member of the gang. Logan was credited with impossible feats of gun handling by eyewitnesses, but it is known by more creditable historians that he easily did the "drop the dollar." Most of his killings, however, were not made in fair fights. His favorite trick was to step out of hiding, jab the muzzle of his gun into the stomach of his victim, and pull the trigger. The Pinkerton files are full of detailed reports on his many murders. He was eventually run to ground by a posse, and shot down in the same spirit in which he lived.

HARVEY LOGAN
An extremely rare photograph

James Butler [Wild Bill] Hickok

Wild Bill Hickok was a bad actor on stage and off. He ranked high among the deadly dandies of his day. Hickok always carried a brace of six-guns in high cavalry-draw scabbards. Frequently they were covered by a wide sash. He was exceptionally fast but fired his guns with only moderate accuracy. For his stage appearances he used smoothbore pistols loaded with birdshot or sand. It's no great trick to break glass balls when shooting at close range with such ammunition. Hickok was typical of the "good" badman of that era. Lawman in one town — wanted in another. He died like many others of his ilk — shot in the back in a Deadwood saloon.

JAMES BUTLER ("WILD BILL") HICKOK
The photo shows Wild Bill wearing a pair of ivory-handled single-action Colts in high scabbards angled for cavalry draw

The Shooting Gallery

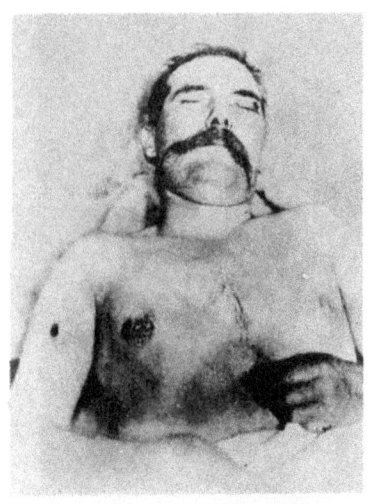

JOHN WESLEY HARDIN
This photo of Hardin was taken shortly after he was shot in the back in El Paso, August 19, 1895

John Wesley Hardin

An unreconstructed rebel, Wes Hardin killed his first man while in his early teens and subsequently blazed a bloody trail throughout the Southwest. One thing that has to be said for him is that he gave his opponents a chance — as much chance as any man would have facing John Wesley Hardin. Like most of the top gun slingers of his time, he favored the high cavalry draw, and often in his later years wore a leather vest upon which the two holsters were sewn. His reputation was such that any man who went up against him was just about licked before he started. Hardin was shot in the back by John Selman, a peace officer who regarded such action as the only sensible way to bring in the greatest gun fighter of them all.

WILLIAM BONNEY
("BILLY THE KID")
The only authenticated picture of Billy the Kid

Billy the Kid

If William Bonney were in action today, he would undoubtedly be adjudged a juvenile delinquent long before his twenty-first year, the age at which he was shot down by Pat Garrett. The Kid was neither all good nor all bad. He was a cold-blooded killer and yet he showed great loyalty to the rancher who befriended him and gave him a chance to go straight. At this man's murder, Billy went on a rampage that wrote the bloodiest page in the history of the Lincoln County War. He was one of the few desperadoes of note who used a double-action revolver, perhaps because he found it faster, or perhaps because the size and shape of the Colt Lighting's butt fitted his smallish hand. More hokum has been written about Billy the Kid than about almost any other man, with the possible exception of the famous William F. "Buffalo Bill" Cody.

However, one fact stands out: his ability to handle a six-gun with deadly effect was great enough to induce Sheriff Pat Garrett — a man of proven courage — to shoot him in a pitch-dark Mexican shanty; to shoot him down without a chance to defend himself.

Ben Thompson

Thompson was one of the most likable men on the frontier, despite the fact that he was an expert and hardened killer. He was considered to be the most deadly man with a six-gun around Dodge City, being both extremely fast and accurate, but his favorite weapon was a double-barreled shotgun. He was murderous when aroused and his reputation for violence almost equaled that of John Wesley Hardin. He was finally ambushed by a rival faction in San Antonio.

BEN THOMPSON
Taken while Ben was City Marshal in Austin, Texas, a position from which he resigned shortly before he was ambushed in the old Jack Harris Theater in San Antonio

Bat Masterson

James Barclay Masterson was a man whose great speed with a handgun, combined with outstanding accuracy, was only surpassed by his great personal popularity. Masterson was a man who much preferred being your friend than your enemy. He often went out of his way to do a kindness for a stranger, and in an era noted for its brutality he got involved in many a gun battle helping out those weaker than himself. He was an outstanding peace officer, and after hanging up his guns, owned a very prosperous bar in Denver. He finally became a newspaperman in New York City.

JAMES BARCLAY ("BAT") MASTERSON
This picture was taken when Bat was a sports editor in New York City, shortly before his death

Luke Short

LUKE SHORT
He was as dapper as he was dangerous

Luke Short was a phenomenon on the frontier. He killed some of the toughest gunmen of his day and never gained a reputation as a top gun. Perhaps his greatest exploit was when he shot and killed long-haired "Texas Jim" Courtwright, one of the most feared gunmen and peace officers from the Lone Star State. The trouble between Courtwright and Short had been brewing for some time and everyone knew that a duel was inevitable. The betting was ten-to-one against Short with no takers on the little gambler. Courtwright was acknowledged the fastest gun in Texas. Short's first bullet nearly severed the thumb from Courtwright's right hand, making it impossible for him to cock his gun. Before he could do the border shift to his left hand, Short calmly took aim and finished him off. It was a severe shock to all Texans. Short died at the age of thirty-nine, a victim of tuberculosis.

Johnny Ringo

Ringo was one of that picturesque breed of post-Civil War southern gentlemen, gone to seed, who wasted their lives in violence. He was an alcoholic — unstable and moody. He carried his .45 in a cross-draw belt scabbard — the only top gun fighter to use an across-the-body draw. He was a gambler and gun fighter and died in drunken violence. There are many versions of his death, but this much is known: his body was found in the crotch of a tree, his boots were off, there was no dirt on his rag-covered feet, and he was dead from a .45 wound. The authorities stated that he had committed suicide in a fit of depression induced by one of his monumental hangovers. Another version is that his drinking crony, Buckskin Frank Leslie, murdered him while he was in a drunken stupor and robbed him of his considerable winnings at poker. I incline to the suicide theory, on the ground that the only man who could be counted on to kill Johnny Ringo was Johnny Ringo himself.

William Tilghman

Bill Tilghman was in fact, for a half century, the sort of fearless, dedicated peace officer who ought to be glorified in Hollywood and on television. He was more than a gun fighter — he brought law and order to Oklahoma to stay. He had great skill with a handgun and was famed as well for being able to hit a man harder with his fists than a mule could kick. He had been a peace officer for more than fifty years when he was killed by a drunken revenue agent whom he had taken into custody; the man pulled a hide-out gun and shot Bill down.

WILLIAM TILGHMAN
"Uncle Billy" probably arrested more desperate outlaws than did any other peace officer

Clay Allison

For pure cussedness, Clay Allison, the club-footed killer, was head and shoulders over his contemporaries. If anything good was ever said of him in print, it was a typographical error. The legend goes that Allison once went to a dentist to have a tooth extracted. The dentist, who was understandably nervous, pulled the wrong tooth. With a howl of rage, Clay leaped from the chair, drew his Colt, and forced the dentist into his own chair, grabbed the dentist's tools, and proceeded to pull all of his teeth. When drunk, he was somewhat of a Dale Carnegie in reverse and a maniacal gun fighter. He would take chances that no sane man would consider. When he died in a fall from a wagon, citizens throughout the Southwest breathed easier.

These men were in my opinion the top gun fighters. Out of these top twelve, only two — Bat Masterson and Wyatt Earp — died of old age. Doc Holliday and Luke Short died of tuberculosis, which seemingly killed more gamblers than did their habit of dealing from the bottom of the deck. Of the remaining eight, Clay Allison and Johnny Ringo died while drunk; Wild Bill Hickok and Wes Hardin were shot in the back; Billy the Kid and Ben Thompson from ambush; Bill Tilghman was killed by a sneak attack; and Harvey Logan was riddled by a posse.

It is more than a coincidence that not one of them was killed in a stand-up shootout. It is impossible to say which one was the best, for none of them ever met his match.

INDEX

INDEX

(Page Numbers in Italics Refer to Illustrations)

accidents, prevention of, 99-101
Ace trigger shoe, *18, 21,* 24, 30, 31, *41,* 49, 55
across-the-body draw, 121, *121*
across-the-body draw holster, 160
action, smoothness of, 26
adapters, grip, 19-20
Agent 2″ Colt, *28*
Agent Special, 22
alley cleaning, 107-08
Allison, Clay, 167, 168
ammunition, 24, 30, 45, 63-72. *See also* cartridge(s).
Ammunition Reloading Handbook, 71
ankle draw, *122,* 123
ankle holster, 73-74, *74*
Armed Forces Police, New York City, 133
armhole holster, 74, *75*
automatics, fast draw for, 128-42

Baretta pistol, 53
barricade shooting, 112, *112*
Bearcat, Ruger, *48,* 49
belt holster, 152
belt pistol, 151
Berns-Martin Speed Holster, 80, 82, 160
Billy the Kid, 164, *164,* 165, 168
bird's-head grip, 25, *31*
Blackhawk, Ruger, 56, *58,* 59
Blue Streak shoulder holster, *79,* 80
Bonney, William (Billy the Kid), 164, *164,* 165, 168

braced shoulder level, in mid-range combat, 111, *111*
Brocius, Curley Bill, 141
Browning, 9-mm., 61
Buntline Scout, Colt, *50*
Buntline Single-Action, long-barreled, 91
Buntline .45 Special, Colt, 56, *57*
Bureau of Narcotics, U.S. Treasury, 102
buscadero rigs, 158, *159*
butts, concealment, 25-26

cartridge(s), .22-caliber, 68-71
　Luger 9-mm., 63
　.357 Magnum, 39
　revolver, *64,* 64-68
　for semi-automatic pistols, 63-64
　Western .38 Super Police, 30
　Western Super X hollow-point, 32, 34
　See also ammunition.
Cassidy, Butch, 163
cavalry draw, 131, *132, 138,* 139-40
cavalry-draw holster, 93, *93*
centerfire hunting weapons, 56-62
Chief Special, Smith & Wesson, *21,* 24, *28,* 30, *30, 31,* 34, 36, 46, 101
Civil War, holsters during, 152, 154, 155
clearing coat, in shoulder draw, *124,* 125
close combat shooting, 102-06
Cobra Special, 22
Cody, William F. (Buffalo Bill), 165

Colt, Sam, 91, 152
Colt .45 ACP bullet, 63, *64*
Colt Agent, *28*, 34
Colt-Astra Cub, 33
Colt Buntline Scout, *50*
Colt Buntline Single-Action, long-barreled, 91
Colt .45 Buntline Special, 56, *57*
Colt Courier .22-caliber, 52
Colt Detective Special, 22, *23*, 24, 26, *28*, 30, 31, 77
Colt "Double Action Lightning," 25
Colt Frontier Scout, 47, 51
Colt Frontier Scout Buntline, 51
Colt Government Model .45 ACP, 32, *38*, 46, 71, 107, 133, *134*
Colt Marshal revolver, 21, 32
Colt #1 National Derringer .41-caliber, *158*
Colt #2 National Derringer .41 rim fire, *158*
Colt Navy, new, *155*
Colt Navy, old, 152, 154, *157*
Colt New Service .357-caliber, 60
Colt New Service .38-caliber, 101
Colt New Service .45-caliber, 29-30, 39, *41*, 43
 formed scabbard for, *81*
Colt Official Police revolver, 17, 21, 30, 37, 40, *42*, *44*, 45, 72
Colt Police Positive Special, 22, 30, 31, 36, *36*, 77
Colt Python, 39, 40, 59, *61*
Colt silhouette target, 95
Colt Single-Action Army Model, 18
Colt .357 Single-Action Frontier, 60
Colt Single Shot, 33
Colt Super .38-caliber, 61, *62*, 63
Colt target hammer, 21
Colt #3 Thuer Derringer First Type .41 rim fire, *158*
Colt #4 Thuer Derringer Second Type .41 rim fire, *158*
Colt Trooper, *44*, 45
Colt Whitneyville Walker, *150*

Colt Woodsman, 53
Colt's Patent Firearms Manufacturing Company, 161
Combat Magnum, Smith & Wesson, 37, *38*, 40, 45
Combat Masterpiece, .22-caliber, 45, *50*, 51
Combat Masterpiece, .38-caliber, 45
combat practice, guns for, 45-48
 targets for, 95-98
combat shooting, close, 102-06
 mid-range, 109-13
 See also shooting.
Commando holster, *88*
commercial targets, 95-98
concealment, weapons for, 29-34
concealment butts, 25-26
concealment holsters, 77-84
Courier .22 Colt, 52
Courtwright, "Texas Jim," 166
cross draw, 91, 142, 155
crossfire holster, *76*
crotch holster, 75, *75*

defense, personal, weapons for, 35-38
Derringer pistol, Remington double-barreled, 33, 34
Detective Series Grips, Herrett's, 19, 49
Detective Special, Colt, 22, *23*, 24, 26, *28*, 30, 31, 77
Dodge, Jess, *92*, *138*
"Double Action Lightning," Colt, 25
Dragoon holster, 89, *90*, 91
 quick draw with, *126*
Dragoon pistol, 152
draw, quick. *See* quick draw.
"drop the dollar" practice, 143, *145*, 146
"drop the hat" practice, 143, *144*
Duramatic, Hi-Standard, 46, 53
Dynamite shoulder holster, *78*, 80

172 Index

Earp, Wyatt, 29, 102, 162, *162*, 167
exhibition right-hip draw, 135

fanning, with Ringo holster, 142, *142*
fast draw. *See* quick draw.
FBI combat training, 102
FBI draw, *118*, 119-20
FBI holster, 160
Federal Speed Scabbard, 79
field holsters, 89-90
Fitz Gunfighter grip, *18*, *30*, 49
Flaig's Ace trigger shoe, *18*, *21*, 24, *30*, *31*, *41*, 49, 55
Frontier Scout, Colt, 47, 51
Frontier Scout Buntline, Colt, 51
Frontier Six-Shooter, 18
fun guns, 49-55

Ganio's .45 Special, *38*
Garrett, Pat, 164, 165
GI holster, 87, 133
"gimmick" holsters, 86, 101, 159, 160
gold block, 22, *23*
Goodhue, "Goody," 26
Government Model .45 ACP, Colt, 32, *38*, 46, 71, 107, 133, *134*
grip adapters, 19-20
grip(s), 19, 20
  bird's-head, 25, *31*
  Fitz Gunfighter, *18*, *30*, 49
Gun Hawk holster, *92*
  exhibition quick draw with, 136, *136*

Half-breed (Outlaw) holster, *93*, 94, 154, 155, 158, 160
hammers, 20-22
hand ejector .32-caliber, 46
Hardin, John Wesley, 94, 139, 164, *164*, 165, 168
Harrington & Richardson top-break revolver, 47
Heavy Duty .38-44, Smith & Wesson 39
Hellstrom, Douglas, 42
Herrett's Detective Series Grips, 19, 49
Herrett's hammer shoe, 22
Hickok, James Butler (Wild Bill), 139, 163, *163*, 168
high cavalry draw, *138*
Highway Patrol holster, 87, *126*, 127, *127*
Hi-Standard Double Nine, *50*, 51, *136*
Hi-Standard Duramatic, 46, 53
Hi-Standard Sentinel, *18*, *19*, 46, *47*, 52, 136, *136*
Holliday, Doc, 102, 139, 155, 162, *162*, 167
holsters, concealment, 77-84
  in fast-draw work, 118-19, 140
  field, 89-90
  "gimmick," 86, 101, 159, 160
  history of, 151-60
  malfunctioning of, 86, 87-88, 100
  ornate, 158
  service, 85-88
  undercover, 73-76, 81
  Western, 91-94
horse pistol, 151, *152*
Hyde, George, 26

"inside-the-pants" holster, 78, 79
  cavalry draw with, 131, *132*
Iver Johnson .22-caliber revolver, 47

James, Jesse, 155
Johnson, Iver, 33
Johnson, Iver, .22-caliber revolver, 47

Keith, Elmer, 56, 71
Keith hand load, *64* 65, *65*
King Ramp Reflector, 24
Kit .22-.32 Smith & Wesson, 46, *48*, 49

Ladysmith, Smith & Wesson, 51
leg holster, 75
Leslie, Buckskin Frank, 166
Llama pistol, 53
Logan, Harvey, 163, *163*, 168
long-range shooting, *114*, 115-16
Loughnan, Thomas B., fast draw of, 133, *134*
low cavalry draw, *138*
low right-hip draw, *126*, 127, *127*
Luger 9-mm. cartridge, 63
Luger Parabellum semi-automatic, *18*, *19*, 46

McGivern, Ed, 113, 116, 159
Magnum Blackhawk, .44-caliber, 40
Magnum .357 cartridge, 39
Magnum revolvers, 24, 32, 37, 40, *40*, 43, 56, *57*, 59, 60, *62*, 64, 71, 113, 115
"Man-Stopper," .38-caliber, 67
Masterson, James Barclay (Bat), 161, 165, *165*, 167
Mershon grip adapter, *18*, 20, 24, *41*, 47
Metropolitan Special, 31
Mexican defense holster, 128
   fast draw with, *129*
mid-range combat, 109-13
Military .44, Smith & Wesson, 39, *41*, 60
Military and Police revolver, Smith & Wesson, 21, *21*, 32, 42, 46
Missouri Skintite holster, *90*, 91, *152*, 154, 155
Model Army .45-caliber, Smith & Wesson, *41*
Myers, "Tio Sam," 160
Myers Border Patrol Holster, 160

National Derringer .41-caliber, Colt #1, *158*
National Derringer .41 rim fire, Colt #2, *158*
Navy Colt, new, *155*

Navy Colt, old, 152, 154, *157*
New Service .357, Colt, 60
New Service .38, Colt, 101
New Service .45, Colt, 29-30, 39, *41*, 43
   formed scabbard for, *81*
NRA Hunter Safety Program, 55

Officers' Model Match, 18, 21, 43, 45, 51
Official Police revolver, 17, 21, 30, 37, 40, *42*, *44*, 45, 51-52, 72
Outdoorsman, Smith & Wesson, 60, *61*, 101
Outlaw holster, *93*, 94, 154, 155, 158, 160

Packmeyer grip adapter, 20
personal defense weapons, 35-38
plinking, 49, 54
pocket pistol, 151, 152, *156*
Police Department, New York, 86, 105
police officer, training of, 147-49
Police Positive Special, 22, 30, 31, 36, *36*, 77
psychology of gun fighting, 147-49
Python, Colt, 39, 40, 59, *61*

quick-draw, 117-46
   for automatics, 128-42
   with revolvers, *118*, 119-27
quick-draw clubs, 146

Ranger holster, *84*
Regulation Police .38, Smith & Wesson, 46
Remington double-barreled Derringer pistol, 33, 34
revolver, quick draw with, *118*, 119-27
   unloading, 100
right-hip draw, exhibition, 135
   low, *126*, 127, *127*

Ringo, Johnny, 142, 166, *166*, 167, 168
Ringo cross draw, 91, 142
Ringo holster, 142, *142*
"rock-the-baby" hold, 110, *110*, 111
Ruger, Bill, 40, 91
Ruger Bearcat, *48*, 49
Ruger Blackhawk, 56, *58*, 59
Ruger .22 Long Rifle Automatic, *52*
Ruger .44 Magnum Super Blackhawk, 56, *58*, 59
Ruger .22 semi-automatic, 46
Ruger single-action .22 Single Six, *18*, *19*, 46, *48*, 49, *60*, 61
Ruger Single Six airweight .22-caliber, 47

safe gun handling, 99-101
Sanderson, Lew, 19
Scabbard, Federal Speed, 79
Seifried, Harry, 19
Selman, John, 164
semi-automatic pistol, accidents involving, 99
service holsters, 85-88
service weapons, 39-44
shooting, close combat, 102-06
 long-range, *114*, 115-16
 See also combat shooting.
Short, Luke, 155, 166, *166*, 167
shoulder draw, 124, *124*, 125
shoulder holsters, 80-81, 155
shoulder level, braced, in mid-range combat, 111, *111*
side-pocket holster, 8-ball, *78*
Siefried, Harry, 52
sights, 22-25, 37
silhouette target, 95, 105, 106, 107
Single-Action Army Model, Colt, 18
single-action draw, *92*, 137, 140, 141, *141*
Single-Action .357 Frontier, Colt, 60
Single Shot, Colt, 33
Six Guns, 71

Skintite holster, 89, *90*, 91, *152*, 154, 155, 158, 160
Smith & Wesson Automatic, 61
Smith & Wesson Chief Special, *21*, 24, *28*, 30, *30*, *31*, 34, 36, 46, 101
Smith & Wesson Combat Magnum, 37, *38*, 40, 45
Smith & Wesson .22 Combat Masterpiece, 45, *50*
Smith & Wesson .38-.44 Heavy Duty, 39
Smith & Wesson .22-.32 Kit, 46, *48*, 49
Smith & Wesson Ladysmith, 51
Smith & Wesson .357 Magnum, 24, 32, 40, 56, *57*, 113
Smith & Wesson .44 Magnum, *40*, 59
Smith & Wesson .44 Military, 39, *41*, 60
Smith & Wesson Military and Police, 21, *21*, 32, *42*, 46
Smith & Wesson Model Army .45-caliber, *41*
Smith & Wesson Outdoorsman, 60, *61*, 101
Smith & Wesson .38 Regulation Police, 46
Smith & Wesson .38 Terrier, 30, *31*, 34, 46
Spatz, Martin, *121*, *125*
spring-clip across-the-body draw holster, 160
Standard .22-caliber, 45-46
Standard .22-.32 Kit gun, 46
Star Model F, 53
stepping coat, in shoulder draw, *124*, 125
Stoeger Arms Corporation, 95
Sturm Ruger Company, 40
Super Blackhawk, 40, 56, *58*, 59, 91
Super Police ammunition, 24, 30
Super Police holster, *84*
Super .38 semi-automatic, 46
super sleuth cross-draw holster, *76*

Index 175

targets, commercial, 95-98
Terrier .38, Smith & Wesson, 30, *31*, 34, 46
Thompson, Ben, 94, 155, 165, *165*, 168
Threepersons, Tom, 160
Thuer Derringer First Type .41 rim fire, Colt #3, *158*
Thuer Derringer Second Type .41 rim fire, Colt #4, *158*
Tilghman, William, 167, *167*, 168
trigger guard, 24, 25, *31*
trigger pull, 26
trigger shoes, 20
Trooper, Colt, *44*, 45
Tyler T adapter, *18*, 20, *21*, *31*

undercover holsters, 73-76, 81
Unique powder, 72
United States Border Patrol, 87, 115

United States Treasury, Bureau of Narcotics of, 102
unloading revolver, 100

Walther models, 32, 53
Webley & Scott .38-caliber, 47
Webley & Scott .455 Irish Constabulary, 32
Western holsters, 91-94
Western Super X hollow-point cartridges, 32, 34
Western .38 Super Police cartridges, 30
Whitneyville Walker Colt, *150*
Winchester Western 200-grain Super Police loads, 40, *65*, *67*
Winchester Western Super-X hi-speed hollow-point .22 Long Rifle, 62
Woodsman, Colt, 53
wrist holster, 74-75, 155

Also Available

CoachwhipBooks.com

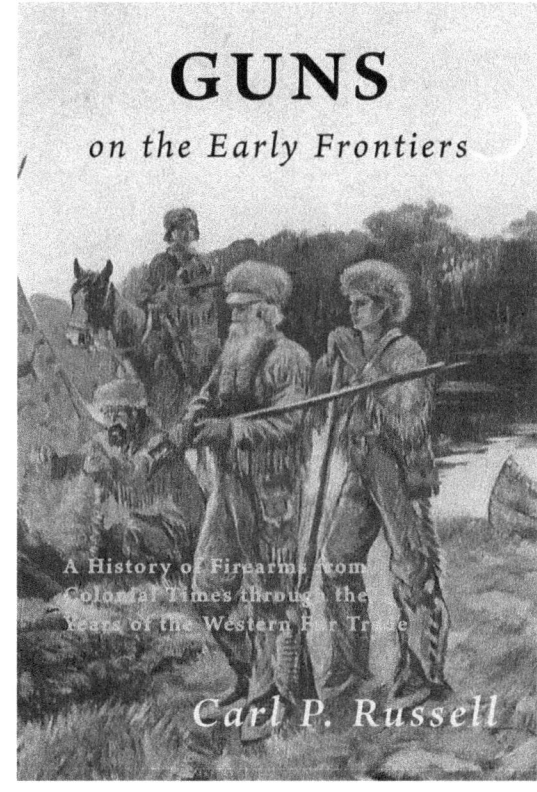

Also Available

CoachwhipBooks.com

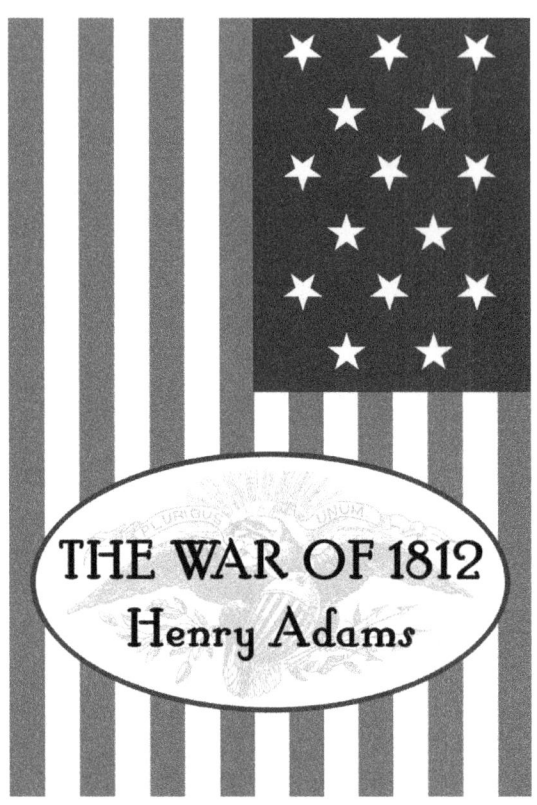

Also Available

CoachwhipBooks.com